D1527559

A DISTURBING INJUSTICE

A DISTURBING INJUSTICE

The true story of a small town doctor and his
battle against an unjust legal system

DR. SCOTT GEISE

CONTENTS

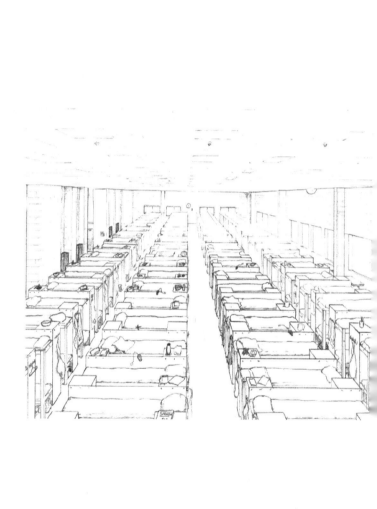

PROLOGUE

Not long ago, I was out for dinner with my wife at one of our favorite Italian restaurants. We sat at the bar enjoying the cozy ambience of the place, the low key buzz of the other diners and the delicious smells of cooking wafting out of the kitchen. As we sipped our glasses of wine while waiting for our table, I noticed a former patient of mine sitting along the bar from us. He'd just ordered a takeout and looked as though he wanted to keep himself to himself so I didn't try to catch his attention to say hi.

My wife and I finished our glasses of wine and the bartender, as attentive as ever, asked, "Dr. Geise, can I get you guys another drink?"

As soon as my name was mentioned, this former patient let out a derisive laugh. Then he jumped up and pushed his chair back so hard it almost fell over. "You're not a doctor anymore!" he yelled. "I read the newspaper and saw you were convicted and sent to prison. You stole from the insurance companies!"

I felt the color drain from my face. I couldn't believe my hardship had caused such irritation in someone I only knew as a patient. "I'm sorry, John (not his real name). But don't believe everything you read in the news. You'd be shocked if you knew what really happened."

With that, John snorted in disgust, quickly finished his

drink and took his food to go without saying another word to us.

~

Many of you who will read this book have known me for years, even decades. When the legal system came crashing down on my life, you probably read some horrible things about me in the newspapers. And though some of you who have followed my story in the media may well think I got my comeuppance, rest assured, you've not heard the whole story.

Sometimes American justice isn't right. Sometimes it goes wrong and becomes deeply un-American.

Just this last summer, while writing this book, I came across an article about the celebrated Pulitzer Prize-winning biographer, Robert Caro. His books chronicling the rise to power of Lyndon Johnson, our 36th president, are not so much centered on the life of the ex-president as on the subject of power and how it works—and more importantly, how power is misused.

Caro was moved to quote Lord Acton's famous axiom, "All power corrupts, absolute power corrupts absolutely." This struck a deep chord within me. Not long after that, I watched a media interview with former US prosecutor Sidney Powell. When I heard her say, "I saw prosecutors make up crimes by piecing parts of two different statutes together and hide evidence that showed people were innocent. Federal prosecutors are absolutely corrupt," my jaw hit the floor.

From my own personal experience with the federal court system, I was beginning to believe this was true.

How is that even possible in America? I asked myself.

I did some more digging and came across an article by Andrew L. Schlafly, Esq., entitled "War on Doctors: Tricks Used in Prosecutions." His first words as to prosecutorial tricks blew my mind. "Show me a man and I'll find you the crime," which was a reference to a popular Soviet Russia slogan about prosecuting innocent people for political reasons.

This was followed by a saying I'd heard over the years—about how easy it was for a prosecutor to persuade a grand jury to indict a person of a crime. I'm sure you've heard it before: "A prosecutor can indict a ham sandwich." The point being, that US prosecutors have virtually unlimited power to indict anyone for anything.

I reference this state of affairs merely as a take-off point. My book doesn't involve the actual political appointment of judges, at least not directly, nor does it finger corrupt FBI agents, but what it does do is highlight how political agendas may drive federal prosecutions, and how wrongly pursued federal prosecutions can upend the lives of good, hardworking Americans such as myself.

Those of you from an older generation may recall with fondness KTAM radio host and icon, Paul Harvey. At noon each weekday, he had a radio show that always began with a short description of some mundane event. Then, right before the advertising break, he'd say, "In a moment . . . the rest of the story."

With thanks to Paul Harvey, that's what I'd like to do here: tell you . . . *the rest of the story*.

CHAPTER ONE

WHITE-OUT

"Integrity is telling myself the truth. And honesty is telling the truth to other people."

- Spencer Johnson

Nobody wins them all. In football, passes are dropped. In basketball, dunks are bungled and foul shots are missed. In the world of sports and life, errors in judgment happen all the time and certainly more often than an athlete would care to admit. I never played professional sports, but I easily suited up and took the field or court—football, basketball, baseball, track, and lacrosse—over 2,000 times in my amateur athletic career.

I was lucky to have been coached by some extraordinary people, men who gave me and my teammates a solid foundation in life. My high school coaches Jim Conley and Jake Villella were two of my favorites, and anyone who follows basketball will know the name, John Beilein. In my sophomore year at Newfane High, I tried out and made Coach Beilein's JV basketball squad, experiencing what it means to be coached by someone truly great.

As a result of that experience, I'm proud to lay claim to having played on one of Coach Beilein's very first basketball teams. As hard as he worked us, to the point of serious pain, we all just worshipped the guy. Sadly, my junior year on Varsity was his last year coaching at the high school level. From there, his career skyrocketed, landing him head coach of the Cleveland Cavaliers and, more recently, the Senior Advisor for Player Development with the Detroit Pistons.

Coach Beilein crowned his high school and college achievements with 12 successful years at the University of Michigan, including nine NCAA tournaments and two runner-up places in the national title game. He is one of only six Division I coaches with 700 or more career wins. As a result, he's widely respected in collegiate sports today as one of the cleanest, most rule-abiding coaches in any sport, something he sincerely preached to all of us who played for him.

Coach Beilein's attention to detail was undeniable, and it influenced us all. He wrote down every statistic from every practice and every game. My high school friend and teammate, Mike Herlan, somehow managed to hold onto the printout he gave to each one of us at the end of our 1977 season. It was Coach's way of showing us where we needed to improve before next season, and we all took that guidance to heart.

There I am, Geise, between Fuller and Hambruch, clocking 18 games played (I played every game that season), with only Hesch and Molisani playing more minutes than me.

(Statistics sheet given to each one of us at the completion of the season)

Coach Beilein made it very clear there were no entitlements in sports or life. If you wanted to achieve your goals, you needed to ignore the noise and focus on your goals until you've achieved them. "Touch every line," he'd remind us as we ran our sprints, making sure we knew how important our own individual efforts were for the team. He drilled into us the importance of situational awareness, of always knowing what was happening around us, such as being ready to help out a fellow player when he's getting beaten to the basket. Always protect your teammates, he preached, just as a soldier must always protect fellow soldiers in the foxholes of war.

Coach Beilein constantly emphasized teamwork. In his eyes, the noblest sacrifice a player can make on the basketball court is to prevent opposing players from driving directly into the basket. He loved it when a player stood his ground and "took one on the chin for the team." Every time this happened, Coach urged the entire bench to stand up and cheer, just as if we'd scored the game-winning basket.

As a young player back in 1976, I took this mission deeply to heart. Taking charges became my addiction, and at age 15 I even absorbed 37 offensive fouls in one season, which taught me a valuable life lesson: no matter how hard or how often you've been hit and knocked to the ground, you must find the courage and stamina to stand back up and continue doing what you know is right.

Even though Coach Beilein moved to the big leagues, he's never been forgotten by his Newfane teams or his local friends. Every year for many decades now, a group of his Western New York followers have come together to visit him wherever he happened to be—not only because he was, and is, an amazing coach, but also because he has helped us, his former players, become the men we are today. We have all moved on with our lives to many different states across this country, but I'm sure we'd all follow him anywhere. Our last trip even took us to Cleveland!

So it was a rare and unique opportunity when, in spring 2017, my former teammates and I prepared to visit Coach Beilein for a reunion and a game in Ann Arbor, Michigan. It was another team effort, with guys joining us from across the country, from Newfane to Connecticut to Texas and California.

Our plan this year was to meet at the hotel, pick up our tickets at the Will Call window that Coach had set aside, watch the game, and then go out to dinner to catch up. As we sat around the dinner table, Coach would focus on each of us in turn, always asking, "so, Scotty Geise, what's happening in your life?" His curiosity was deep and authentic, and everyone would listen, like kids sitting around a campfire, utterly engaged. He paid rapt attention to our answers and would occasionally interject a probing question or an insightful observation, sometimes with a chuckle. And he always seemed quietly yet inscrutably buoyed by our news.

Funny how half a lifetime had passed since he'd coached us, and yet each of us would try to impress him with our achievements. That's what great mentors do, right? They encourage you to pursue excellence in everything and always have the most insightful advice. They give you the tools and the discipline and the rigor of achievement. But, most important of all, they ignite the belief in you that you can achieve anything so long as you train hard, work as a team, and stay clean.

Playing sports taught me honest hard work always pays off and that there are no shortcuts. The crazy story of this book notwithstanding, that's how I've always tried to live my life. Although, as events turned out, maybe this belief and trust in America's institutions were somewhat naïve—because I was placing trust in a government that, at least in part, landed me in such serious trouble later in life that it rattled my belief in America.

As always, the drive out to the game was great fun, filled with lively locker room banter as we regaled each other with familiar stories from our glory days on and off the field. But after an hour of catching up on stories the car fell silent. We'd been getting along just fine, even famously, but there was still the Elephant in the Highlander—the elephant that for over a year had worn a green prison jumpsuit. Finally, one of the guys cleared his throat and tested the water. "Scott, I hope you don't mind me asking, and tell me to mind my own beeswax, if you like, but, look, we all saw the newspapers back when you got arrested. What the heck happened there? Did you really spend time in prison?"

Even though I knew someone might ask, there's no way to prepare for this question coming at you from the small confines of a car. There was no place to run and no place to hide and no way to dodge the question. My face must have turned five shades of crimson, as I felt the heat explode off my back and neck. Even though I had already owned it big time for years, very few people knew the whole story. "Yeah, buddy," I said. "I'm glad you asked."

Except at that exact moment, before I could say another word, we hit a total white-out. I couldn't see a thing. Not the car in front of me. Not the side of the road. Nothing. How we didn't meet our maker that day, I'll never know, but by some miracle, I managed to stop the car and avoid colliding with the car in front of us by mere inches.

"Ah, Jesus," I said. "There's been an accident up ahead. It's going to be slow going for miles. Just look at it."

There was a pause, then one of the other guys said, "Scott, you were saying?"

"Yeah," I sighed. "And since it looks like we're going to have plenty of time for me to tell you *the whole story*, I may as well start at the very beginning."

CHAPTER TWO

GROWING UP GEISE

"When everything goes to hell, the people who stand by you without flinching—they are your family."

- Jim Butcher

If you look at a map of New York State, find the point where Lake Erie dumps over Niagara Falls, and go east for 18 miles to the shores of Lake Ontario, you'll stumble upon the quaint little town of Newfane. It's here I was born Scott Daniel Moon and grew up in a tight-knit community of Irish, Dutch, and Italian immigrants. Although back in 1830 its population was only 1,430, through slow and steady growth, that number had ballooned to 9,000 by the early 60s when my older brother Steve and I entered the world.

I have no memories of my original namesake and biological father, Laverne Moon. During some very hard times, when Steve and I were still very young, apparently he packed up his bags and left town. At least that's what I was told. Since I was only one at the time, I have no memories of him at all. Over the years, I've often wondered what kind of man he was and why he thought it necessary to walk away from his entire family in the abrupt way he did. Unfortunately, I've never gotten the answers, or, at least, anything more than superficial ones.

The older I got, the less I really wanted to ask, and to Steve and I, it didn't really matter.

My mom, Shirley, was the youngest girl in a family of seven sisters and two brothers. She grew up during the Great Depression, when most families were still struggling financially, and she worked hard for everything they had. Shirley's father, my grandpa Stevens, had died when Mom was only four years old, leaving to her mother, Gertrude, the task of raising the entire family on her own. Naturally, in those difficult times, everyone pulled together to survive, and it was commonplace for our older siblings to mother the younger ones. Even after all the children married and had children of their own, many stayed locally in Newfane, showing how close-knit the family was.

Mom met and eventually married Richard Geise, who had grown up in the Finger Lakes region close to where I would later go to college. Going by the name Dick, he'd left the small town of Manchester and arrived in Newfane in 1962. Soon after they met, they decided to get married, and Steve and I even participated in their wedding. Fortunately, Laverne had waived his parental rights before leaving town, thus allowing Dick to adopt us. He's still the only person we've ever called Dad.

I don't think my brother and I would have turned out the way we did had the remaining Moons not embraced our new dad so warmly, allowing him to take a genuine interest in us. When the adoption proceedings finally went through, and Steve and I legally became Geises, the whole Moon family—including my grandmother, Edith Moon, my aunt Cheryl, and my aunt Karen—all embraced us as if it had never been any other way. In other words, we became one big melting pot of three families, and it has been amazing ever since.

As it turned out, Dad also came from a large family, with one sister and five brothers. As this was the norm in those days, it wasn't long before I had two younger brothers, Mark and Matt. Of course, there's a big difference between a biological father and a real dad, and I was very fortunate to be raised by the latter. And throughout all my legal hardships, I did everything I could to be the same involved, loving dad to my own three sons as he was to me.

We grew up in a large house on North Main Street, directly across from Rutland Funeral Home, within walking distance from school and all the other activities that four young boys could dream up.

Mom and Dad were active and highly respected members of the Newfane community, and that inevitably rubbed off on us. Years later, when I was building my dental practice, I made a huge effort to throw myself into community projects, not only because it generated business but also because making a positive contribution to the town was just what you did as a Geise. You rolled up your sleeves and you joined in. That was the glue that held families and communities together.

The Methodist church was also a central part of our lives growing up. It was just four doors away, and the old cobblestone Baptist church was adjacent to it. Everything was close by, so we walked to Boy Scouts, Sunday school, and church in a matter of minutes, and we attended all sorts of festivals and gatherings throughout the years, from hunting for Easter Eggs to the Fourth of July celebrations.

All my brothers and I, and most of our friends, wound up joining the Boy Scouts. As such, we planned fundraisers and camping trips and learned how to contribute to an organization. We all worked together and realized early on that you need to respect the people around you if you're going to accomplish anything in life.

Throughout the school year, it was quite normal for at least one of us to have an extracurricular activity, but living close by certainly made it easier for our parents. We had marching orders every day: walk straight home, put our things away, do our homework, and then, and only then, could we change into play clothes and venture back outside to play or go to the family room to watch our favorite shows – *Batman*, *Superman*, or Westerns such as *The Rifleman* and *Bonanza.*

We spent hour after hour playing sandlot football or baseball after school in the summer sun and because Newfane was a small town, and everyone was related to everyone else, it was common after the games for someone to say, "Hey, you wanna come over for dinner?" This would immediately spark a phone call between moms to make sure it was okay, as respect and trust were the words of the day, and we never allowed ourselves to disobey that.

My parents were proud of their own house, too. They were always doing something to improve things for us, whether it was wallpapering a room or fixing up our bedrooms. Between the two of them, they didn't have a whole lot of extra money, but we made do with what we had, and everyone was expected to help out whenever needed. As boys, we mowed lawns and did odd jobs throughout the neighborhood. Most of our neighbors were elderly, and they always needed something done around their homes too. This early work ethic earned us a few extra bucks here and there, so we didn't have to ask our parents for money. Newfane was a real-life "Mayberry R.F.D." located in the wilderness of upper western New York, a quiet town where family and neighborhood came first, and everyone helped each other out.

Regarding our family of four boys, I was the second oldest, and there were three years between me and my next younger brother, Mark, and five years between myself and the youngest brother, Matt. And, of course, there was our big brother, Steve. Growing up with three brothers, we tried every sport, and everything in our house had to be competitive, from cards to Monopoly to even tree climbing.

Sixteen months older than me, Steve was my hero growing up. He still is. Even though I have always looked up to him, I also wanted to compete with him, because he was always stronger. Not so much faster, but definitely stronger. No matter what we were playing, everyone wanted Steve on their team, because it wasn't fun getting beaten up and then losing too. He played with so much heart that you would have thought there was a Superbowl trophy on the line every game. If ever I had to be placed in a foxhole with just one soldier, and it was do-or-die time against ridiculous odds, my choice of soldier would be obvious.

Life as an adult is of course very different from life as a kid, and our parents rarely told us if they were struggling with medical problems or just plain old life problems. We were protected from the vast majority of that, but, as we all know, hardship can strike at any moment, especially when you least expect it.

CHAPTER THREE

AN EARLY LIFE LESSON

"Life is partly what we make it, and partly what it is made by the friends we choose."

- Tennessee Williams

There was no town police force in Newfane. Everyone looked out for each other, and crime was nonexistent. Should the rare defalcation arise, the County Sheriff dealt with it kindly and humanely.

Our neighborhood was a mix of many nationalities, but that didn't matter because everyone was family-oriented and community-minded. It was a fantastic place to grow up, but this was nothing special. Newfane was—and is—like many other small towns in America of that era.

Everyone was friends and neighbors, which could be good or bad. If we as kids got in trouble at school or displayed poor manners, our parents would greet us at the door with full knowledge of what we'd done. Nobody got away with anything. Walking home from school took us past the homes of various family relatives who would often step outside to say hello or, if we were really lucky, to give us chocolate chip cookies, that's if Aunt Jean, Aunt Mary, or Aunt Joan, was baking that day. Everyone on this path was loving, with watchful and protective eyes.

When I veered off that path one cold day on my way home, I paid dearly for it, learning a lesson I'd never forget. Peter L., a friend from class, happened to be walking close by, and he started to tell me about something funny that had happened to him that day at school. He was a good laugh, but not one of the close friends I usually hung out with.

Peter was on his way to Clark's Feed Store, where he'd spend time after school sweeping out the shop, stocking the shelves, and starting up the trucks when it started to get cold outside. I could see the building easily from my own backyard, an old wooden structure from Newfane's Electric Railroad days, and Peter wanted to stop by the store to get some salt licks for his pet rabbits, which he said the owner, Mr. Clark, had given him for helping out.

As we walked along East Avenue, Peter got more and more excited about me visiting "Clarkie." When we arrived, he walked up to the front door and found it was locked. He seemed surprised at it being closed, so he moved over to the window and put his hands on the lower sill. "Clarkie must have forgotten I was coming," he said. "But I'm going to use the secret entrance. You coming?"

Yeah sure, I thought, as I had no idea what Mr. Clark allowed Peter to do or not to do and assumed whatever Peter wanted to do was OK. I just knew I wasn't going inside without Mr. Clark there. After staying outside for what seemed like ages, I was about to turn for home when Peter finally emerged from the window, blithely stuffing a salt lick in his pocket and jingling a set of keys.

He walked directly toward one of the old dump trucks parked in the yard, climbed inside the cab, started the engine, jumped out of the cab, and moved a lever on the side of the back bed. The bed started to rise into position to dump something, but then he let go of the lever.

"What are you doing?" I asked.

"Clarkie lets me start the engines on cold days like today and then play around a little. Wanna see a can get crushed?"

"Sure," I replied.

When Peter placed an empty cola can just beneath the raised bed and lowered the lever, I watched in amazement as the six-inch tall aluminum can was flattened to a paper-thin wafer in moments.

"That was cool," said Peter. "You wanna try it?"

"No thanks," I replied. "I should really be getting on home. See you tomorrow."

By the time I'd walked the short distance through the field and into my own backyard, the extended family grapevine was already buzzing. My mom's eldest sister, Aunt Scottie, who happened to work at the Newfane Fuel Depot, right next door to the feed store, was already in on the scoop, as her only window looked right onto the yard.

Unbeknown to me, as Peter had stepped through the window, she must have looked up to see him going in and me standing by like a lookout. She had immediately phoned my mother at her work to tell her, and my mother had, in turn, phoned my father and told him to meet her back home as soon as possible.

Unaware of the tightening grapevine around me, when I got home I rushed through some math homework, put everything away, and had just changed into my play clothes when I heard the sound of someone arriving downstairs.

"Scott, can you come down here please!" Dad yelled. Though I sensed something was up, still I didn't know a small jury of adults had hastily assembled at the bottom of the stairs. Mom and Aunt Scottie were talking softly to each other, and Dad was standing there with a very concerned look on his face. I could see I was in trouble.

"What did you do after school today?" asked Mom pointedly.

"Ah, uh, I walked home with Peter, and we stopped for a couple of minutes at the feed store," I said, answering truthfully but not fully, as I knew better than to lie outright.

"What were you doing over there?" Mom said. "Were you guys playing with the trucks?" Already she looked on the verge of tears.

"Yes, Peter was showing me how he crushed cans and—"

As soon as those words left my mouth, Dad gripped the hair on the top of my head and directed me back up the stairs toward my bedroom. He would never hurt us, but he had no qualms about being firm if we deserved it.

I swear I could hear Dad's teeth clenching as we climbed the stairs (which immediately makes me think of *occlusal guards*—my nemesis—but all of that will become clear later). He was muttering something I couldn't understand, but I could clearly hear the disappointment in his tone. When we reached my bedroom, he let go of my hair and stared at me.

"I'm so mad and disappointed in you, Scott! Why did you steal from Mr. Clark? We taught you better than that!"

Trying not to cry, I said, "but Dad, I didn't take

anything from Mr. Clark."

"Aunt Scottie was right next door," he snapped. "She saw what you were doing."

I knew better than to talk back, especially at a moment like this, so I stayed quiet.

Grimacing with anger, Dad continued. "I'm so, so, so mad right now. You're grounded . . . forever!" he yelled, then stormed downstairs.

Right then and there, my whole world collapsed. Disappointing my parents was bad enough, but not being able to play outside after school was inconceivable. I closed my eyes and tried to picture the truck yard to figure out what Aunt Scottie would have seen from her vantage point. Maybe she hadn't told them I had stayed outside, or maybe she wasn't looking because she was on the phone. Either way, the way I saw it, my life was over.

"I didn't go inside," I yelled at the top of my lungs. "Peter just took a bunny lick for his rabbit."

I didn't want Peter to get into trouble, but the bunny lick was the only thing that could have been taken, unless, maybe, Mr. Clark was saving those aluminum cans for something. Either way, I knew I hadn't taken part in it.

Mortified, I curled up on my bed and ran my mind over what had just happened, wondering whether I would ever see the light of day again. It had been a normal walk home, I told myself. And yes, the stop at the feed store was unusual, but Peter worked there or at least seemed to hang out there a lot with the consent of the owner.

Even though I had never done anything remotely like this in the past, much less anything illegal, ever, I realized it only takes one accusation to turn your entire world upside down.

Someone must have heard the last words I yelled out because soon there was a big commotion, and people were talking quite heatedly. When Mr. Clark arrived, I could hear a muffled version of everyone discussing what Peter had done. The horrible feeling of being wrongly accused made me sick to my stomach.

Aunt Scottie obviously only saw part of what happened. Making things worse, Mom and Dad believed her partial account was the full account. Even though I was only 11 years old, I could not understand why everyone was presuming me guilty without first getting my side of the story.

For what seemed like hours, I lay in bed as the heated discussions continued downstairs. Finally, the house went quiet, and I heard Dad's footsteps trudging up the stairs. I steeled myself for another telling-off, but, when he entered my bedroom, I could see his demeanor had changed.

His anger and disappointment had been replaced by something I had never seen before. With tears forming in his eyes, he said, "we talked a little more with Aunt Scottie, and she did say you never went inside the store. Mr. Clark also said he lets Peter work the trucks, but Peter shouldn't have entered through the window without him there."

There was a long pause, and then he continued. "I'm so sorry we didn't listen to your side of the story before drawing our conclusions. You've always shown you know right from wrong, and you've always made us very proud because of it. I hope you'll forgive me for getting so angry."

I remained silent as Dad hugged me and added,

"you're not grounded. In fact, I'm the one who should be grounded for not trusting you."

Before leaving the room, he ruffled my hair affectionately and gave me a reassuring smile. I lay on my bed for at least another hour, missing dinner and spending the rest of the evening upstairs. I couldn't shake the sick feeling of being wrongly accused.

The next day, I tried to pretend it had never happened and went about my normal routine. Then, for the remainder of my high school years, I never allowed myself to be caught in a situation like that again.

Moreover, I pledged, from that point forward, I would only trust my true friends and steer clear of everybody else.

CHAPTER FOUR

HOBART COLLEGE

"There are no guarantees in life. The simple twists of fate and the breaks of the game are the two maxims that define so much of the success and failure in life."

- Bill Walton

I always knew I would go to college. Even from a very young age, I wanted to do something special, so I applied to several colleges before I began my senior year in high school. I'd also done really well in interscholastic sports and wanted to continue playing at the college level, and maybe beyond.

By pure chance, Hobart's quarterback, Pat Tumulty, came to work out with our high school team during the summer of 1978, and we soon became good friends. One day, as we were passing the ball at practice, he told me he would be a senior next year, and that he believed I was good enough to play wide receiver immediately as a freshman there.

I wanted to stay relatively close to Newfane, and Hobart College was just two hours away, so I applied and was fortunate enough to be accepted. And like any other kid heading off to college, I had tons of dreams and goals but I also wanted to pay my own way through. I wasn't getting any sports scholarship offers from any of the larger schools, so financial aid was going to be challenging.

Hobart was a small Division III school and they did not offer athletic scholarships so I couldn't rely on my athletic abilities to help pay for my education. The school did assure me I'd be able to apply for a grant-in-aid scholarship, and the sports programs would help me in any way they could. Part of my financial aid package involved a job on campus washing dishes in the Gulick dining hall and eating for free once the plates were clean.

So in the fall of 1979, I became a Hobart Statesman, and it turned out to be an absolutely incredible experience. First and foremost, playing on a college sports team affords an instant camaraderie which makes the transition to college easy and exciting. And because I was fast, tall, and solid, I had size on most of the league's defensive backs and was able to earn a starting position pretty quickly.

My high school guidance counselor pushed me toward studying engineering because I had done really well in both math and science, but I still wasn't quite sure what I wanted to do on the academic side of things. But the best part was I was now playing college football, and all I wanted to do was catch footballs, score touchdowns, and win games. I felt like I was on a team with my brothers again.

Unfortunately, I didn't have a very successful season that first year, as the team employed more of a "run-first" offense, which didn't give me many opportunities to do what I loved, which was to get the football into my own hands. I soon saw my dream of going to the pros falling apart.

After my first football season ended, I was also doubting my choice to pursue engineering. I was taking a couple of biology courses and was enjoying them so much that I decided to take more. Also, around this time, because I didn't have anything going on, sports-wise, the football coach, who also happened to coach the lacrosse team, urged me to give the sport a try. Coach Urick, who was inducted into the National Lacrosse Hall of Fame in 1998, gave me my first lacrosse stick and had me play catch off the gym wall as often as I could, and I would be invited to try out the following fall with the now reigning National Championship Team. As it turned out, I loved the game, and after running my heart out in try-outs, applying everything tactical I knew from basketball and other sports I had played, I was beyond excited when I found out I had made the team.

As soon as my Sophomore year football season ended, lacrosse season began. We had some pretty incredible games against some pretty incredible teams, and we went on to win the Division III National Championship again that spring. But even though I was having the time of my life in lacrosse, my heart was still centered on excelling in football.

I also decided that I was going to stick with my new major in biology. I didn't know what I was going to do with a biology degree, but I knew for sure I wasn't an engineer. One of my dearest friends, Heather B., who was also my girlfriend at the time, was a biology major, and her father, Dr. B, happened to be a dentist. She encouraged me to speak with him, and he's the one who ultimately got me interested in dentistry.

The more I got to know him, the more I wanted to

follow in his footsteps. Soon I set my mind on getting into dental school and started to schedule all the prerequisite courses so I could apply.

I also set my mind on finishing out my senior year in football by training harder than I ever had. I had a talk with my brother Steve, and neither one of us was going to be denied. We had heard stories of Earl Campbell running up and down sand dunes in army boots to develop the tree trunk legs he had, so we thought we could do something similar. We didn't have any sand dunes in Newfane, so, to train, we decided to use the car as our workout platform.

We would jump into our old Ford Maverick, the same car our Grandmother Moon gave us when she passed away, drive it out to one of the country roads, shut the engine off, and place the car in neutral. We pushed plenty of cars out of the snow during our winter months in New York, and if you have ever had the pleasure of doing so, you know how difficult that can be.

Our preferred workout method was to have one guy sitting in the driver's seat to steer while the other pushed hard until the odometer moved to our goal. Then we'd switch and continue, over and over again. Many of the local residents stopped to ask if we needed help. We kindly refused, and, when they drove off, we looked at each other as if to say, well, we might not have needed it physically, but mentally it was a whole other story.

~

So in my final year at Hobart, through a series of twists and turns and a new freshman quarterback, I began to catch a lot more footballs. The new quarterback, Tommy, and I had good chemistry and together developed such a great strategy that we started to destroy our opposition.

That is why I would say, don't ever give up on a dream because they do come true, eventually. By the end of my senior year, I had broken every receiving record at Hobart.

(Post-game press interview on Boswell Field with the Democrat & Chronicle reporter, myself and Coach Daniels)

And if that wasn't thrilling enough, I soon learned I had made the All-American Football squad along with my brother Steve who was studying at Upper Iowa University. Two Geises on the All-American Football squad made for one very happy Geise family and plenty more material to add to Mom's scrapbook.

By the time lacrosse season rolled around, I was still scrambling to finish my last biology courses so I could graduate. To apply to dental school, I also had to take the

DAT (Dental Admission Test), which measures aptitude for handling all the dental school course load. I had no other option but to schedule the test on the morning of the first intercollegiate game ever played in the Carrier Dome in Syracuse, and I had to take that test before meeting up with the rest of the team. I remember Coach Urick trying to relieve my stress by telling me my DAT was much more important than anything else going on that day.

The test was long and tough, but I made it back to the Carrier Dome by halftime, with my parents, my Uncle Butch, and Grandma Geise all waiting in the stands to see me play. Having lost to Hobart in 1982, Syracuse got its revenge that day, beating us 17–10 and going on to win their first Division I National Championship.

We played on to win our fourth straight Division III National Championship that year, and every year from then on in the 1980s. Hobart achieved a record 12 consecutive national championships, which started my freshman year, and which to this day is more than any other school in any other sport in US history.

My four years at Hobart were some of the most incredible of my life, with many great memories and invaluable friendships that remain to this day. Some people say life is a series of choices, and sometimes you have to make sure you're going in the right direction by getting on the right bus. You might think I was leading a charmed life, but when I chose to attend Hobart College, I definitely boarded the right bus.

When the end of my senior year finally came, I was able to graduate with a Bachelor of Science Degree in Biology. Despite doing really well on the DAT test, I would still need to wait a whole year before being admitted into dental school. This gave me a unique chance to explore football as a possible career.

Sadly, even though I landed myself a try out with the Buffalo Bills, I tore the rotator cuff in my left shoulder during try outs, which put a sudden end to my long held childhood dream. When the team doc heard I was planning on going to dental school he took me to one side and administered a painful dose of reality. "Listen, kid," he said. "Don't ruin your health playing football; if you have a chance to go to dental school, take it. You'd be a fool to get yourself hurt by coming into this league when you have an opportunity to become a dentist." Then, looking me square in the eye, he intoned one last time, with sobering finality: "Go—to—school."

As disappointing as it was, I took his advice and even though my life hadn't quite gone the way I'd hoped or planned, I did have a new goal and I couldn't wait to begin studying for an exciting new career in dentistry.

CHAPTER FIVE

DENTAL SCHOOL

"A dream does not become reality through magic; it takes sweat, determination, and hard work."

- Colin Powell

I realized my hard academic work was finally paying off when, after applying to three dental schools, I was fortunate enough to get accepted by all three of them.

The University of Buffalo School of Dental Medicine was always my first choice, mostly because it was a state school with cheaper tuition for residents and fairly close to home. Buffalo also enjoyed an excellent reputation and has always been ranked as one of the top schools in the nation.

The first couple of years were intense. As a class, we were thrown straight into demanding courses such as Gross Human Anatomy, where six of us were able to share the experience of dissecting a donated cadaver. We also shared many classes with the medical students through our freshman and sophomore years, but, as dental students, we were assigned additional lab projects that added a significant amount of extra time in the school.

I'm not going to lie; it was hardcore in those early years. We students had to immerse ourselves in all the projects and materials, with little time for anything else.

It seemed unrelenting, and the pace really didn't slow down until the third year, when we began to see patients clinically, cleaning their teeth and learning about overall patient care.

Before I started, both the dental and medical schools had been expanding into extra space, with construction going on everywhere. But come my junior year, the shiny and beautifully equipped Squire Hall opened up on the south campus. Overjoyed, I was fortunate enough to be in the second class graduating from this extraordinary new facility that incorporated into its curriculum the latest in scientific dentistry.

Besides the new facility, we had some excellent professors and mentors. The faculty members were also fantastic and wanted very much for their students to appreciate that they were valued members of the school. Although they stressed "that you weren't a doctor until you were a doctor," the instructors made you feel comfortable, and were very much in your corner, willing to help out in any way they could.

In my senior year, we had a competition for the best "crown and bridge" work performed by a student. These restorations are called "fixed" prosthodontics because they are glued in place, and I had replaced the front six teeth for one of my patients. There was also a competition for the best "removable" appliance—removable because they can be taken out of the mouth whenever needed—and I had made a brand new set of dentures for another patient. I entered these patients into each of the contests, and, when the winners were announced, I was pleased to take second place in both categories, fixed and removable. Always competitive, I do remember murmering to myself as I went to collect the award, "always the bridesmaid, never the bride!"

Finally, after four long years of dental study, I passed my board exams and was ready to graduate. The school appreciated the enormous accomplishment involved and always put on a fancy show at graduation time. There the esteemed instructors who all have a clutch of different degrees wore vivid tassels, ribbons, and fur to match their robes. It was an awe-inspiring and colorful experience that made me proud to be included in their world—finally, as Dr. Scott Geise.

Mom and Dad were there with happy tears of pride because I was the first member of the Geise family to graduate as a doctor. Because my achievement involved an incredible amount of time and energy, I was relieved, excited, and emotionally exhausted, but I was also on a huge high. And it was great because all my siblings and the many members of my extended family were there to celebrate my success.

And just like that, I was officially a 1988 graduate of the University of Buffalo School of Dental Medicine.

CHAPTER SIX

MILITARY

"Don't count the days, make the days count."
- Muhammad Ali

With dental school behind me, I did something few other dental graduates do: I fulfilled another goal in life and volunteered for the US Army. The decision sadly meant having a heart-to-heart talk with my girlfriend. Heather was great. She understood what my leaving the country for three years would mean, so we decided to end our relationship as very dear friends, and we still are to this day. Most of my classmates probably thought I was crazy, but importantly, my family didn't.

I could have volunteered for the Army before dental school, and, if I had, the government would have paid for my education, but they also wanted two years of service for every year they financed school, and that was too much for me to commit to. So I refused to take a path that would have locked me into eight years of military service. Also, I had already made a deal with my hometown dentist to join him and eventually buy out his practice. As he was the only dentist in my small hometown of Newfane, I didn't want to jeopardize that opportunity, so a three-year tour of duty (ideally overseas) was the perfect filler.

I was informed by the Army recruiter of the opportunity for a placement close to Frankfurt, Germany. This sounded ideal, so I signed on the dotted line, received my commission, and soon I was headed to Fort Sam Houston in San Antonio, Texas (named for the US senator and first president of the Republic of Texas, Sam Houston), to go through basic training in the summer of 1988.

Basic training is no piece of cake and within a day of being there, I was selected to lead my platoon, overseeing around 45 other healthcare recruits on a nine-week course. During the week, we had PT (physical training) every morning at Zero Dark Thirty and then classes both morning and afternoon. I learned a lot in a very short time and left San Antonio in the best shape of my life, ready for just about anything. Upon completion of basic, my MOS (mission occupational specialty) was 63 Alpha, which is Army lingo for a dentist.

Next stop: a small base in Hanau, Germany, for the next three years, as Captain Scott Geise.

I loved being in Europe, with every new destination a brand-new adventure. Assigned to the New Argonner Dental Clinic, I was able to learn and work alongside eight other dentists, gaining enormous experience. To be close to work, I lived off base in the third-floor apartment of a German family's home. I made sure to integrate myself into the local culture and felt very comfortable there, but I did return home once for my 10-year high school reunion in July 1989, with my commander's gracious permission, of course.

As soon as I arrived home, I embraced my parents and spent the first night with them. I also did my best to catch up with my high school buddies. Out of all the people I was hoping to see at the reunion, I was really looking forward to reconnecting with my best friend, Mike Molisani "Monk". He was in love, and he had let me know he was engaged to be married, so we were really excited to get back together and catch up on what was happening in our lives.

The next night, on July 15, 1989, I had made arrangements to meet him in Lockport, at the most happening place at the time, a place called Faces. He was in Jamestown that afternoon with two other guys, David Hesch, also from our high school basketball team, and another guy from the class behind us, Eric Lohnes. Eric had just picked up his brand-new car the day before, a sparkling red Grand Prix.

On their way home to Lockport to meet me, something went terribly wrong. Eric lost control of the vehicle, crashing into a parked car, and killing all three of them. I waited all night for them. There were no cell phones at the time, so I just figured there must have been a change of plans, and I would catch up with Monk in the morning. I went to bed expecting to do just that.

I can still see the white, shocked faces of Mom and Dad as they broke the news to me the following morning.

"Scott, I'm afraid we have something terrible to tell you. Monk and Dave Hesch were killed in a car accident last night, along with Eric Lohnes."

I couldn't believe what I was hearing. It couldn't be true. I got myself up and dressed and went directly to the Molisani's house, only to find them in a state of utter anguish. Mrs. Molisani managed to tell me what had happened but I still couldn't take it in. Monk was her eldest of four boys. Dave Hesch was also the eldest of four boys, and I could only imagine that the Hesch house was in just as much shock and pain as this one.

After doing what I could to help the Molisanis that fateful day, I was asked by the family to speak at Monk's funeral, along with Jim Weber, their next-door neighbor. Our high school friends were still our best friends those 10 years later, and we had lost them, just like that. Monk and Dave are on the left-hand side of our team photo.

J. V. Basketball
Boasts a 15-3 Record

J. V. BASKETBALL CHEERLEADERS Row 1 M. Dominick Row 2 L. J. Bernecker, J. Dorney, G. Denny, S. Harrington Row 3 D. Stevenson, R. Schultz, K. Sweeney

This year's Junior Varsity Basketball team finished with the best record in 8 years, 15 wins and only 3 losses. Sophomores Dave Hesch, Scott Geise and Mike Molisani played vital roles in this successful season. Freshmen Jim Weber, Jeff Currie and John Hambruch, to name a few gave the team added support and all appear to be on their way to fine careers.

J. V. BASKETBALL Row 1 J. Weber, D. Lukasik, J. Hambruch, S. Geise Row 2 M. Molisani, D. Hesch, M. Herlan, C. Porter, M. Ramsdell, J. Currie, J. Phipps, N. Fuller, M. Royer

91

(Page from the 1977 Newfane Central Schools yearbook)

Even today, as I head to and from work in Buffalo, I drive past the spot where they were killed and can't help but look over to see what never should have happened.

We had a very somber reunion that year, but before I returned to duty in Germany, my closest friends and I talked about doing something in memorial for those guys, our friends who had so much more to give. One night, after I returned to Germany, Jim Weber, Charlie Porter, and Mike Herlan met at the Willowbrook Golf Course and had a couple of beers at the old barn. During their conversation, Web coined the phrase "Friendship Memorial Golf Tournament," and they began laying plans for the first tourney to be played in 1990.

Since that time, that tournament has been held every single year, and we have never had a rainout since. It has raised money for high school scholarships in the names of each of the three guys, presented at an awards ceremony before graduation, and given to a high school senior demonstrating the qualities of each of those guys.

In all, $150,000 has been raised, with donations going to local needs such as the local hospital, the Diabetes Foundation, and other local organizations that needed support. Then, in 2002, we began giving out $500 to three students each year who exemplified the characteristics of each of our fallen friends. Today, as our balance has grown, we now give $1500 to each of the three students in the hope their college experiences will make a difference, all in the names of our friends.

Our Friendship Memorial Tournament is played on the third Saturday in July every year, without fail, and it has kept all our families extremely close even to this day.

Experiencing loss in such a brutal and sudden way is enough to change anyone's perspective on life. And so it was that at 27 years of age, I found myself living in Europe, practicing as an Army dentist, knowing that time is short, and anything can happen to anyone at any time.

My brilliant solution was to travel all over Europe, see *all* the sites, and broaden my horizons. I met another dentist, Chip Clayton, who became my constant travel companion. I'm not exaggerating when I say we attended nearly every festival in Europe over those three years.

Since Europe and the rest of the world were pretty peaceful at the time, I never felt in any danger, even during a trip to Berlin just before the wall came down.

I remember when President Reagan gave his famous 1987 speech at the Brandenburg Gate, in Berlin. "Mr. Gorbachev," he said. "Tear down this wall!" I was at the Brandenburg Gate just a year later and I acquired some huge chunks of the concrete and had them shipped home to hoard a piece of history. To this day, a massive 50-pound piece of concrete covered in dull blue and black graffiti with the number 88, presumably to reflect the year 1988, takes pride of place in my house. Eighty-eight was also my football number at Hobart, which is perhaps why that particular chunk caught my eye.

August 1989 - Photo taken by Chip Clayton just after I yelled
"Freibier Heute!" through the opening

During those years, I also visited Greece each summer
and spent time on some of the coastal islands, using up
every last day of my leave time. I didn't save a dime. I
spent every last cent on adventures, such as skiing all over
the Alps with the Frankfurt ski club or traveling to Paris,
Amsterdam, Venice, and loads of other exciting European
tourist hubs. I knew I'd never get a chance to do that
again, so I went at it hard and met so many incredible
people from each country. And I've always followed the
Golden Rule. People are people, and when you treat

others the way you'd like to be treated, with respect and dignity, life is amazing.

But it wasn't all just fun and games, I loved my work too. I was assigned to the 26th Support Battalion and spent time with them in the field, taking care of any dental problems the soldiers might have. Also during that time, I trained with them as well, and the opportunity presented itself to participate in the EFMB, the Expert Field Medical Badge (really the only specialized training available to the medical service corps).

It was a grueling three-day test, with events such as disassembling and assembling an M16 rifle, effectively lifting the wounded out of M1 tanks and onto Blackhawk helicopters, and transporting a wounded soldier through simulated battlegrounds.

Amazingly, I made it through, achieved my badge, and was selected to participate in a very select training for a group of health professionals. It was a Special Forces course to provide hands-on training for Advanced Trauma Life Support. I can't tell you how we got that hands-on training, but I can tell you it was the most incredible weekend of instruction ever. Surgeons from the Navy and Special Forces medics from all services were there, and I was able to gain so much knowledge from them. Unbelievable!

By the time I was finally finishing up my tour in Germany, I received the Army Commendation Medal for meritorious achievement, and I was able to leave there with absolutely no regrets and a lifetime's worth of memories. *Danke schön*, US Army!

CHAPTER SEVEN

RETURN TO NEWFANE

"Where you go when you leave isn't as important as where you go when you come home."

- Lindsay Eagar

After the military and three years traveling Europe, it was time to return to Newfane to reconnect with my family and begin my career. That meant working as a dentist for Dr. Jim H and hopefully finding a beautiful woman with whom to settle down and raise a family.

My parents were still there, and I was now 30 years old. I had put my student loans in forbearance, so there was no repayment during the three years I spent in the Army. But, when I got home, I had to start paying them off while investing the rest of my time and money into buying Dr. H's practice.

There's no other way to put it, except to say Dr. H was a difficult man to work for. I liked him a lot, but he felt he set the benchmark for dentistry in Western New York. In fact, he thought he was the best at everything, whether it was mountain biking, chess, drinking, or whatever you could conjure up in your head. Jim's personality was Alpha Male all the way, so working for him and then alongside him was challenging, to say the least. As an associate, my number one goal was to build up the practice and serve as many people in the community as I could. It was now 1992, and I knew if I was to make this thing work, I was going to have to strap my boots back on each and every day.

Jim and I were stuffed into a tiny office building of only 960 square feet, and so it became a constant challenge for two dentists to work efficiently in the confines of that small space. And not only two dentists but of course, two dental hygienists as well—all crammed into this little area. To this day, I still own that same building and have rented it out to other professionals. It's part of the medical complex I've always dreamt about building to help improve downtown Newfane.

Having been away from Newfane for 11 years, I made a point of joining every organization that would take me as a member, to reintroduce myself into the community as far and wide as I could. I was a member of the Newfane Lion's Club and a board member of the local hospital, and I signed up for various charities: you name it, I was on it. I did everything I could to put myself out there, letting everyone know I was home to make a difference.

I also involved myself in numerous projects with my alma mater, Newfane High School. I was part of the Allied Health Program, mentoring kids interested in dental school or advising them on what to expect in a professional, academic setting. Naturally, I was very active with the sports teams and helped the coaches and the teams in any way I could.

I was out there, engaged in the community and spreading myself all over the place, so, within about four years, I had doubled the practice size by bringing in more and more patients. Dr. H was unable to keep up with my pace and wanted to retire, so he began to take increasing amounts of time off work, gradually transitioning his patients to me and allowing me to use both operatories at the same time.

Slowly I started to buy him out of the practice. It was a crazy time because we were so busy, and our waiting room just couldn't cope. In the end, it was great training and helped me truly understand the business side of dentistry, but I knew I needed an ambitious long-term solution that involved something much bigger and better for my patients and the community as a whole.

CHAPTER EIGHT

TIME TO SETTLE DOWN

"Romantic love is only an illusion. A story one makes up in one's mind about another person."

- Virginia Woolf

My childhood dream had always been to go to college, achieve success, then come back to Newfane, have a family, and raise my kids there as my parents had done. When I met Lizz, we hit it off right away, and I was driven to get married and realize my dream. Love is blind, of course, as dreams can be, and I won't beat around the bush any longer in saying I was just plain ready to settle down.

My good friends tried to slow me down a bit, but I was stubborn in my betrothal pursuit. My best friend, Monk, never had the opportunity to start a family, and that was weighing pretty heavily on my mind. After just a few months of dating, I proposed. Lizz said yes, and we were married a year later. Looking back, it was all a bit quick. I may have traveled the world, but clearly, I was still emotionally quite immature and didn't do my due diligence.

Lizz also came from a large family, and her parents had divorced when she was little, so we shared a similar upbringing. Although her father lived in town, she never had much of a relationship with him, something that was still riding heavily in the back of my mind. And then, to top this off, she shared similar entrepreneurial aspirations with dreams of opening her own salon. She had worked for different companies demonstrating hair products and was very successful at what she did. I had hoped we could work together toward success, but that didn't happen. I needed someone to be on my team and supportive, and that didn't happen either.

I thought we were doing just fine, at least in the beginning, but I was working hard with a blinkered vision of what I wanted our business to become, and maybe she thought I wasn't paying her enough attention. My main goal was to get my new practice running, and so I spent every moment managing my patient load within the tight, and often stressful, confines of that little building.

We welcomed our first son in December 1996, and I was overjoyed. There was nothing more beautiful than that little boy, well at least not until we had our second son in 1998. There was no doubt we were extremely busy, but I tried to be the best dad and husband I could possibly be, not only caring for the boys but also being involved with everything in the house. It's a funny thing when new parents have a child. They don't realize that it's a game of two on one until the second child comes along, and then it's one on one. In 2000, to my total joy, we had our third son, and now we were forced to play zone defense, and that's when teamwork really came into play.

So by the year 2000, we had a family of three amazing boys, and I was well into the planning portion of expanding Newfane Family Dentistry. I was particularly aware that I couldn't handle the stress of a small office much longer. I was always preoccupied with business concerns, and I know that started to hurt my marriage. I didn't notice what was happening at the time. It just crept up on us, and, before we knew it, we had drifted too far apart.

We were living in Lockport, but my goal was to raise my family in Newfane, close to my office, something that became somewhat of a contentious issue between my wife and me. I wanted my boys to have the same fantastic experience I had growing up in a very quaint and loving town, and that's where my goal of creating something special enters the story.

CHAPTER NINE

THE DREAM OFFICE

"The best years of your life are the ones in which you decide your problems are your own . . . You realize that you control your own destiny."
- Albert Ellis

When Dr. H began talking more and more about retirement, and I finally owned the practice outright, I knew I either needed to add on to the existing building or acquire another location. We had made it work in the tiny space, stumbling over each other notwithstanding, but it made things much more stressful than they needed to be.

Downtown Newfane was never a planned business community. It was more like a mixed-use, proto-residential business area. There were several businesses and then a house or government building and then another house or two, in no particular order and following no particular logic.

Alongside our dental office at 2733 Main Street was a big house owned by Max Hughes and his wife, Grace. Max and I had become pretty good friends. He knew of Laverne, something he mentioned once, but never elaborated on. Instead, he always praised my parents, Shirley and Dick, for all they did for his own kids and grandchildren during their time at the high school. He had been struggling with some respiratory and other health issues, but we would bump into each other as I was leaving work. (Just imagine a guy hiding behind his garage, sneaking a cigarette so his wife wouldn't catch him!)

One time, Max beckoned me over and said, "Listen, you know I'm having some health problems, and Grace isn't going to be able to handle the big house all by herself. Maybe if you're going to expand, you should just purchase this house and the whole property and move forward in that way."

He made the same suggestion on several occasions over the years as he enjoyed a clandestine smoke. He was a straight-up honest man and a frank talker. "Hey," he'd say if I hesitated, "I know I'm not gonna be here forever. And you know, you're a local kid. I'd love to be able to help you out. If we can sell the house to you for a reasonable price, so that Grace can be well off enough financially, it would be great for all of us."

Sadly, in the summer of 1999, Max quietly passed away. When the time was appropriate, I approached Grace about buying the house from her, but she didn't want to sell. Grace said the house contained all the memories of her life with Max, and that, as long as her health allowed, she would try to stay there. I began to wonder if Max had actually told her about his concerns for her, or his discussions with me for that matter. But I totally understood her sentiments and realized I needed to start looking elsewhere in the community for a suitable building.

During my search, I learned Castle's Restaurant was

shutting down and that the building was coming up at auction. It wasn't the perfect site for me, just to the north of town, but Castle's had a sentimental value as it was the first job I worked while in high school. Unfortunately, when I attended the auction, another buyer was much more interested in the property than I was, so I let it go. It worked out fine because it kept me looking for a better opportunity and a much better fit for what I had planned. It's just a funny memory now, and I guess it set the stage for what was to come.

As I continued my search for a larger property, providence shone down. The Maytag Appliance store, just three doors away from me at 2727 Main Street, came up for sale. It was a 4,000-square-foot cinder block building, four times the area of my previous office, easily big enough for what I needed, and conveniently just a short walk down the street. The building had an open floor plan with no dividing walls, so I could create any interior configuration I desired. In short, it was perfect—close to my current office but also right on Main Street downtown. It had the added benefit, or possibly damaging element, that I could be the on-site project manager between juggling my patient load.

Before closing on the building, I signed up for a two-day course in dental office design, which turned out to be one of the best investments I ever made. The course was taught by architects who covered everything from ergonomic office positioning to efficient transitions between treatment rooms. Efficient workflow to comfortably handle more patients in the same amount of space was paramount. The building I was about to buy was perfect, and after nine years of fixing teeth in a crawl space, I was able to design a flawless dental *palazzo* that has stood the test of time.

With that purchase also came another—a small house at 2729 Main Street, that I planned to knock down to create the dental office parking lot. I also planned to move the entrance from the Main Street side of the building to the south side so patients could enter from the new parking lot. My plans got underway in the summer/fall of 2000 when I hired my friend, and one of my former employers, Bruce Barnes, to start work on the building. Good things were finally happening, and we made fast progress on the structure. I also was bringing in more money because Dr. H was taking even more time off, which enabled me to buy him out completely and use more of my earnings to fund the construction. I had to push off paying down my student loans a little bit further, but it was well worth it.

Even though I was very careful to make sure all construction work respected my neighbors, the activity must finally have been too much for Grace next door. She asked me to stop by one day, and I was all ready to apologize for anything that was bothering her. To my surprise, she began by telling me how proud she was of the work I was doing and then asked if I was still interested in buying her house. Her family had found her a smaller apartment close by them, and Grace was excited about making the move. So, as fate would have it, I had now been granted the opportunity to create a downtown plaza by owning all properties between 2727 and 2733 Main Street. Weirdly, at this point in my life, I had owned a total of three houses and had to make the gut-wrenching decision to tear two of them down.

The building construction continued to run smoothly until, by the spring of 2001, we were nearing completion, with only the parking lot and sidewalks up to the building to finish. I had already contracted with another lifelong friend to complete the project. His family had a successful construction firm specializing in excavation, concrete work, and outdoor structures like pole barns. He had already started work on the parking lot when one of my hygienists, Wendy Fazzolari, approached me and asked if I would consider allowing her husband, Tony, to do the sidewalks as a way of enabling them to pay for some dental work I had done for Tony the summer before.

A dental issue had been making him pretty self-conscious of his smile, so I went out of the way to accommodate him during his weekly schedule by seeing him on the weekends. All had gone well until it came time to pay for the service. I always gave my employees a small discount, but these particular services required external laboratory work, so I had to pass at least those charges on to Tony, meaning he had an outstanding balance with me that Wendy now wanted to take care of.

Wendy was a fairly attractive woman, and a good hygienist, but had an extremely poor attitude with the other employees at the office, always making the other women feel inferior to her. Tony was about 5'10" and wore his long dark hair pulled back into a ponytail. He was a likable guy and a bit of a schmoozer, but I knew him to be hardworking and competent. In July 2000, when my son Thorne was born in Lockport Memorial Hospital, Wendy had been down the hall giving birth to her own daughter. There was no doubt that at this point in time, we all got on pretty well.

Tony was a Union Laborer for Local 91 out of Niagara Falls and was opening his own business. I had no idea a union contractor could open his own business, especially in the same trade of concrete, but that was none of my concern. When Wendy approached me and said, "Hey, my husband's starting a business doing concrete work. Can he do the sidewalks to pay off his bill?" I said, "Sure, I think that'll work out. But I'll need to talk it over with Buddy first."

When I broached the subject with my contractor, he didn't like it at all. And when I tried to explain it was the only way Tony could pay me back for his dental work, he honored my decision but was obviously offended. Later, he even pulled his entire family from my practice. I felt terrible since he was doing such a great job, and he had completed everything else but the sidewalks. It wasn't a great decision on my part to lose an entire family just to make it easier for an employee, but I felt sure the disgruntled family would come to their senses and return. As a result, Tony paid off his bill by doing the work in the spring of 2001, just a short time before we were due to open. I still have the receipt showing I paid for all the concrete and other expenses, and Tony simply supplied his labor for free.

Wendy obviously felt the time was right to ask for more favors. She made it clear she and Tony wanted to pay for their niece's braces (I had already started her treatment). In fact, I had received the first $50 payment from Tony's sister, Gina. To inform Gina of Tony and Wendy's generosity, I instructed my office staff to do a credit adjustment and send the $50 back to her. I was already giving this family a sizeable discount for their daughter's case simply because she was one of the very first I had treated, and, to make the cost even more affordable, I extended those payments out over five years. Not a bad deal. The total bill amounted to $1,500. From then on, Wendy assured me she would take care of things directly with the front office staff and work out the financial arrangements with them. I trusted her, as I would any friend or employee, to make good on her word.

Finally, after years of planning, saving, and hard work, we sent out invitations and posted notices for our grand opening, and it was a smash hit with the people of Newfane. In fact, the development was so ambitious and expensive a Buffalo business journal even ran a piece on me in June 2001, declaring my $750,000 to $1 million project on Main Street, Newfane "is making Dr. Scott Geise the biggest private developer in the Niagara County hamlet in decades." I was quoted as saying, "I can't remember any other project like this in my lifetime."

Before this, absolutely nothing had ever changed on Main Street, apart from an occasional business change within a block. Most of the buildings were falling into disrepair, and there was really no reason to invest in these structures without an interest in the area itself. I already had that interest, but the future of Newfane was dependent upon getting others interested as well.

New energy within the community was evident almost immediately, and pride in the town was growing. That would be a great summary of Newfane, because the Pride of our Town was all about "growing." Orchards and farms were everywhere. My soon-to-be ex-wife didn't refer to it as "New Farm" for nothing.

I formally dedicated the new dental office I had built

to my parents—two people who had dedicated their entire lives to their growing family. They were thrilled and beyond emotional. Friends and family alike filled the waiting room and spilled outside into the parking lot. There was standing room only. The local senator attended the event and declared the project to be an excellent improvement for downtown Newfane. This was a massive milestone in my career and for me personally. I was bursting with pride, but the achievement was much bigger than mine. My development was subsequently credited with kick-starting the revitalization of Newfane's South Main Street.

In the center of the parking lot where Max's house at 2731 had once stood, I had a gazebo built within a 3,200 square-foot park, with terraced landscaping and benches, so the area could be used as a community space, which I have made available for weddings, concerts, and all kinds of special public events ever since. I have never charged a cent for the park or gazebo's use, and I continue to pay for all the upkeep to ensure it's kept available for the community's benefit. Each spring, we purchase hanging baskets to accentuate its beauty. I pay for all the landscaping that's done there, and I personally initiated the Newfane Concert Series that occurs there every Wednesday night throughout the summer. This gives musicians the chance to perform in front of townspeople who want to enjoy an evening on Main Street.

Every fall, the Newfane Sidewalk Festival invades my entire parking lot and property for the benefit of both the vendors and the shoppers. Every Christmas, we light up the beautiful evergreen that burgeons on the gazebo property. My family and I have decorated the gazebo with

Christmas lights, a Santa sleigh, and other costly decorations that most people take for granted. We even invited Santa Claus into my office each year so children could tell him their Christmas wishes.

On the floor of that gazebo are inscribed the names of my three incredible sons, "The Geise Boys, Stone, Myles, and Thorne."

The waiting room of the dental practice was fitted out with large arches and Greek columns, inspired by my travels around Southern Europe. The dental office resembles a Mediterranean villa, except it's filled with state-of-the-art equipment. Newfane had never seen anything like it. You wouldn't know it from the outside, but, when you walked inside, you were immediately enveloped in a relaxed, comfortable atmosphere, something especially important for a dental office. And the feeling of light, air, and space was so refreshing to my staff after being cramped into two tiny operatories for nine years.

I was 39 years old, and I felt at the top of my game. I had made a giant splash. I had finally arrived. I was smashing records all over again, and the future looked bright for my family, my community, and career.

Had I grown too big for my boots?

Was destiny leading me inevitably toward a fall?

I honestly had no inkling that, within a few short years, everything I had worked so hard for would be in jeopardy, and that I would be forced to embark on a desperate fight to protect first my livelihood, then my reputation . . . and lastly my precious liberty.

CHAPTER TEN

9/11

"If we learn nothing else from this tragedy, we learn that life is short and there is no time for hate."
- Sandy Dahl, wife of Flight 93 Pilot

After the grand opening, we worked hard throughout the summer to bring in new patients. The spanking new modern facility created an opportunity to serve our expanding patient base better, defray the cost of expansion, and enhance salaries for everyone. This enthusiasm and joy carried over until that fateful morning on September 11, 2001, when Islamic terrorists hijacked four planes and crash-attacked the Twin Towers.

The tragedy of 9/11 entered even closer to my little world at about 9:28 a.m. Eastern Standard Time. My assistant nervously entered the operatory room where I was in the middle of placing some fillings. I stopped what I was doing, and, when I looked over at her, the wild look in her eyes immediately told me something was terribly wrong. "Dr. Geise," she said, "you won't believe it, but a plane has hit the Pentagon." That was uniquely disturbing news because my brother Steve was currently working at the Pentagon, a fact that was known in the office.

I excused myself and rushed out to find out if he was safe, praying that whatever had occurred didn't include him. I didn't know precisely where he was, only that he was in the Pentagon somewhere. I called the only number I had for his office phone, but there was no answer. I called again and again, getting more and more frantic until someone answered.

"Major Douglas here."

"Major, this is Dr. Scott Geise, Major Geise's brother. I am aware of the attack there, and I'm very concerned about my brother. Have you seen him?"

"Sir, we're addressing the situation now, but I can tell you I know Major Geise, and I just saw him five minutes ago. He's helping with rescue operations in the impact zone. It was a horrible crash. People are everywhere. I'll let him know you called."

"Thank you, Major Douglas, carry on, and we're all thinking of you here."

I immediately called my parents, who were undoubtedly in shock as well, and let them know Steve was alive and that I would get more information from him when I could. Then I returned to my patients a bit rattled and apologized for my sudden absence. Thankfully, right before midnight that night, Steve reached me on my home phone. Standing there, in a state of disbelief, I was relieved and yet horrified to learn he had escaped harm by the thinnest of margins, as the plane had hit the ground first and then bounced upward and out above the third level. Call it what you will—a twist of fate, luck, divine intervention—because Steve was supposed to be on the third floor when the huge commercial liner (American Airlines Flight 77) hammered into it, exploding in a giant ball of flames.

I learned there were 189 deaths at the Pentagon site—

125 in the Pentagon building and 64 on board the aircraft. Usually, 22,000 people work in the Pentagon, but, on that fateful day, there were only 18,000 because employees had not yet returned to their offices following a recent renovation. But Steve's fate was fickler than that. As Head of Army Operations—his final job at the Pentagon—he was scheduled to head to a meeting at the Big Room in the Wedge. When he arrived 15 minutes early, however, he decided to step out into the courtyard outside the third tier to have a cigarette. The irony is that, for years, I'd been urging him to quit smoking because, as the package says, "Smoking Kills." Thank God he hadn't listened to me, yet.

The Pentagon took a hit that day but was rebuilt in less than a year, proving the steel, resilience, and resolve of the American people. The National 9/11 Pentagon Memorial was completed in 2008, creating a quiet escape for those wishing to pay their respects to those who died at the Pentagon at 9:37 a.m., EST, September 11, 2001. There's a plaque displayed at the memorial donated by Newfane Family Dentistry and Dr. Geise.

Since that time, Steve, his wife Dee, and I have donated to the Wounded Warrior Project because, as they say, every warrior has a next mission. More than 52,000 servicemen and women have been physically injured in our nation's most recent conflicts, with another half a million living with wounds invisible to the naked eye. The Wounded Warrior Project addresses these issues, and I can't think of a better way to help than to give to this great organization.

As a nation, only 1 percent of our population ever serves in the military, and I'm extremely proud to say I was a part of that elite 1 percent.

CHAPTER ELEVEN

CHALLENGES

"To be tested is good. The challenged life may be the best therapist."

- Gail Sheehy

In Spring 2002, I received notice from Hobart College that I was being inducted into the school's Athletic Hall of Fame that fall. All my hard work on the football and lacrosse fields had paid off. This was something I had dreamed about every time I stepped onto that field.

My entire family, my parents, my brothers, and their wives, a whole bunch of friends, and my own three boys were there to join me for an unbelievable weekend. And, to top that off, as unbelievable as it may seem, just one week later, I traveled with my parents out to Fayette, Iowa, to see Steve get inducted into Upper Iowa University's Athletic Hall of Fame too.

As Geise boys, we couldn't have been prouder.

But even when you feel you're on top of the world, you never know what life will throw at you, and, over the subsequent years, my new dental office definitely encountered some challenges. At first, it was all about getting the new equipment installed and operating as it should. There's a learning curve with everything new, with all the structural changes, but these were particularly trying times because we were in the middle of the computer revolution. The majority of my staff was stubbornly against computers. It took putting everyone through classes—hygienists, assistants, front desk people—to make the transition. The pushback lasted a couple of years, but over time everything got sorted.

Now that Dr. H had completely retired, I needed another dentist for my expanding practice. My other best friend had also recently married, and his wife was a dentist who had, like me, trained at the University at Buffalo Dental School. Since graduating, she had been working as a lecturer for a Buffalo dental technology company; she wasn't enjoying it, which created an opportunity for both of us.

I couldn't think of a better way to help a lifelong friend than to bring his wife, a recently graduated dentist, into the mix. I'd always heard, and believed, that it's bad business to hire family or friends, but my relationship with them was strong and transparent, and our frequent discussions about our future plans were all out on the table. We met often and discussed all our concerns.

Our friendship grew even stronger because of it, and my hopes for the future were finally coming together. He and I had been great friends ever since kindergarten, and he was like a brother to me. We both had two people stand up for us as best men at our weddings. He had been one of the best men at my first marriage, and I had been one of the best men at his. He was godfather to my eldest son, and, in turn, I was godfather to his eldest daughter. So you could say we were pretty close.

By hiring his wife, whom I will from this point forward refer to as my Associate, I hoped I could share my success with them. I was a Newfane guy, and she was a Wilson woman. It was only a 10-minute drive between the two places, and because there wasn't a solid dental practice in Wilson, by bringing her on board, we would get a lock on all the patients in that area—a sound business proposal if ever there was.

Unfortunately, it wasn't long before I noticed my new dentist simply wanted to take my runoff, rather than bring in new patients of her own. From my perspective, I saw someone unwilling to go out there and help build the practice, as I had done so diligently when I first started. Soon I started to believe she was simply coasting along, taking advantage of an easy opportunity.

My associate had no ownership of the practice, but she was essentially given the entire overflow in a very busy and growing patient base. All new patients were allowed to become her patients exclusively. The vast majority of the new patients were arriving at Newfane Family Dentistry, not because she was a bright young dentist but because they had been referred to us by other satisfied patients of mine.

I had made it crystal clear from the very beginning that she was to become involved with community organizations and introduce herself to the area through involvement, and, in this way, she could begin to develop her own patient base. All practice owners bring on associates to do the same thing, to find a capable dentist to buy them out at retirement or find a capable dentist to work alongside and grow a practice for their mutual benefit.

A solo dentist who's doing everything right and has a thriving practice still needs an influx of new patients to replace those who move away or naturally pass away. As older patients leave this world, other young patients are needed to take their place; otherwise, practices die along with them.

Therefore, in a situation where no one's planning on retiring soon, associates need to bring in patients to fill their own books, without relying upon the new patient referrals the owner gets. When I bought out Dr. H, I had to do it this way, as do the vast majority of practice owners across the nation.

The friction was not intolerable at this early stage, to be sure, but it was a distinct point of contention. A young, progressive business owner wants to grow a business, not rest on his laurels. Further complicating the situation was that her husband and I had such a long friendship together.

For whatever reason, my associate didn't involve herself in the Newfane community. As she had grown up in the neighboring town of Wilson, I assumed she would at least try and promote herself there. We mutually agreed that, if things didn't work out for her in Newfane, she could easily develop a patient base for herself in Wilson. She was from a very large and reputable family, so it shouldn't have been a difficult thing for her to achieve. However, on top of putting no effort into growing my practice, she wanted to become a partner within just a few short years. I had already paid my dues over the last decade, so to speak, and she hadn't even started yet, so I allowed her to once again prove her worth to the practice.

Besides being stressed over this business relationship, my own marriage had become extremely difficult—so much so that Lizz and I divorced in May 2003, after nine years of marriage. We had tried everything we could to stay together, but, even after many sessions of marriage counseling, we felt living apart was the right thing for our boys.

It was a heartbreaking decision for me because I knew, once we separated, I was going to lose time with my boys, an inconceivable thought while they were still so young. We shared custody, so naturally, I got to spend half the time with them, but that was still devastating to me. It must have been equally hard for Lizz too, but trying to run a business and raise a family as a single father wasn't easy.

We're on good terms now, and I don't regret anything because we produced three amazing kids. I couldn't be prouder of the fact I have three unbelievable sons from that marriage. I'm absolutely beyond thrilled with how each of them has handled that divorce, and how they have all matured into kind, intelligent, and successful young men.

One evening in 2004, I ran into one of my old mentors, coach Jake Villella, and, from his complexion, I could tell he wasn't doing so well. His wife filled me in and let me know he was struggling every day just to get out of bed. I decided there and then I needed to do something that should have been done years earlier.

I began working directly with the Newfane High School athletic department, and it didn't take me long to organize a dedication of the high school track to Jake. The school had absolutely no funding available, but they loved the idea of dedicating the track and field records board to him as the "Father of the Newfane Track and Field

Program."

I worked with a local sign manufacturer to develop a lighted board for all of the individual and team records for both the boys' and girls' track programs, and we all set up a date for the grand dedication. Jake and his family were invited to a track meet in the summer of 2004, where I was personally able to speak for the man who had made such an impact on my own life and the lives of so many others.

It was a very emotional day for everyone involved. He was beyond thankful, and his family continues to thank me to this day. Jake Villella, my teacher, coach, and friend, died of cancer that fall.

CHAPTER TWELVE

BETRAYAL

"The saddest thing about betrayal is that it never comes from your enemies."

- Unknown

I took umbrage at the notion of my associate's fast-tracking because it had taken me 10 years to buy into Dr. H's practice and expand it into the successful business it was. I had also just invested close to a million dollars in building my new facility, specifically designed to work best with two doctors. Yet, here was a young dentist who wanted her chunk after only a few years and who had done little more than take as much as she could.

My philosophy was simple: before a new dentist could become an owner, s/he had to show me that s/he was going to do something to help diligently grow the practice. And if not, then they would have to remain on as an employee—an associate. *You can't just take my patients,* was my thinking; *you should be building your own book of business.* And that was the point of contention that became divisive. Sadly, with division arises suspicion.

During the coming years, I would find her falling behind in her daily schedule. *What is she doing?* I would ask myself. *Your patients are here; go get your patients.*

Don't make them wait longer than necessary, because, in the business of dentistry, no one likes to wait any longer than they need to, especially when they're feeling uncomfortable to begin with. I made it a point to ensure all patients were seen on time, and no one would have to wait for more than a few minutes, unlike most other medical practices, where an hour wait before being seen was commonplace.

The most frequent breakers of this rule were the two veteran hygienists, Wendy and her best friend Julie, along with my associate. And here's where I'd add the irritated edge to the narrative in my mind: *I don't want our patients waiting anxiously to be seen while you guys gossip about what's going on in town.*

I viewed it harshly, as a matter of professionalism. You know, you're a doctor, so you have to act like a doctor. Especially if you're aspiring to be a partner, don't act like you're an employee punching a clock, with nothing deeper at stake. If you want to become a partner quickly, set yourself apart and lead by example. All of this kind of thinking is the product of divisiveness: you get critical. A spinoff to this was the well-worn refrain, as applied to patients and clients—you can't be friends with everyone—which many a business pundit might have told me was my first mistake.

One problem begets another—another truism that applies here. My associate wasn't feeling good about things either. She was complaining, with increasing bitterness, that the front desk staff weren't treating her like a doctor. She openly complained about my office manager at Newfane Family Dentistry, who just happened to be my ex-sister-in-law. She was responsible for the smooth running and efficiency of all activities in the office and was well aware of the office policy to not keep patients waiting, as such she could see the lack of respect for this policy shown by my associates, Wendy, and Julie. As might be predicted, this tension eventually took a toll.

I had never asked my new dentist to sign a noncompete (which is found in virtually all dental practice agreements) because I never had a problem with her practicing anywhere other than this little town of Newfane. We talked and went back and forth on things, and I let her know I wanted her to be successful, but it shouldn't be all on me. She seemed to agree, as it made total sense: why would any dentist bring in a new dentist who could take his clients and open up another practice down the street? That was inconceivable to me.

Instead, as I later learned, she was in discussions with both her patients and one of my hygienists, Wendy Fazzolari. Her patients, of course, were actually my patients, but I didn't get wind of this early on. If I had known she was telling my patients she was going to leave and urging them to go with her, I would have let her go the day I learned about it. But I didn't know about it, and she stayed on and continued to recruit, apparently telling them of her plans to open up her own practice in Newfane, *right up the street.*

We were now heading into 2005, and there's a word for how I ultimately felt. That word is betrayal. At first, of course, I didn't think that way at all, knowing that, as humans, we don't always see things the same and don't always agree. Sure, I would have preferred someone to come on board as I had come on board, bringing in new patients, working 24/7 as it were, with the plan to be there for decades. My investment in the Newfane community certainly proved where my heart was. But there came a point where I could no longer turn a blind eye. I could no longer view recent events in any terms other than betrayal.

This realization was not the solution. It only put a level of emotion on the subject that made finding a resolution even harder. So, during the final months of 2004, all I heard were rumors that a dentist under my own roof was building a new practice elsewhere, but I didn't know where. I was busier than hell, and so, despite hearing the rumors, I chose not to believe them. I assumed that if she wanted to leave, she would come to me and tell me, "Scott, it's not working out, and I feel I need to start my own practice elsewhere."

The source of the rumors was not the office; it was people from out and about in the town. Remember, I was born here. My family—parents, children, pets—were from Newfane. Everyone knew the Geises, so I was approached from all over the place: at games, restaurants, cafes, and shops. Suddenly, people were coming up to me in town telling me what they had heard and asking if it was true. It was a small town and, as such, was not exempt from small-town gossip. The Newfane grapevine was buzzing with the rumor that someone had purchased a restaurant a mile and a half up the road from my office, but I didn't immediately make the connection with my associate because I didn't believe she would do such a thing.

About a month before Christmas 2004, a sharper point was put on the situation. She came up to me one night, just as I had finished up with my last patient. "Listen, Scott," she said, "before you hear from somebody else, I want you to know I have decided to start my own practice."

So, the rumors were true, I thought, my heart sinking. "Where will your new practice be?" I asked.

To my astonishment, she had indeed bought that same restaurant and planned to open up her practice down the road from mine. A wave of hurt and anger flared inside me. "What the hell?" I said, "I thought we were all friends and we'd talked about this. You know I would give you my blessing if you wanted to go off on your own, despite my disappointment. I really would." As a friend, whose husband was one of my very best friends, I sincerely wanted her to be successful.

But I didn't want it to be at my expense. I didn't want to feel betrayed. "If you set up down the road like that," I stammered, "all you're doing is taking patients away from my practice here in Newfane, a practice that I have built up over 13 years."

I couldn't fathom what I was hearing, but it was all true. The whole situation seemed inconceivable to me, especially as she knew I would need to hire another dentist to handle the size of my practice. Her patients, of course, were 100 percent patients of Newfane Family Dentistry.

I took a deep breath. "In light of what you have just told me," I said as calmly as I could. "I can't let you stay here and work for my practice and then just steal my patients when you eventually leave. If you think you deserve that, you're, you're . . . crazy." I knew it would take her months to complete her new office. I had already been through all of that, so I had no choice but to say: "You're fired!"

I just couldn't see it any other way, but I was also acutely aware of our friendship, and I was already thinking ahead. "Listen," I said, "we've always had a great relationship. I hope we can stay that way. But if you take any of my patients or my staff, I'm going to have a very, very big problem with that. That's not just building your own practice but taking from me what I've built up through years of toil. And if you do plan to do this, it's going to be difficult to continue being friends with you guys. I sincerely don't want to see that happening. So please, respect what I've done here when you leave. That's all I ask."

But, unfortunately, that's not what happened. In spring 2005, about five months later, and before my associate opened up her new place, Wendy Fazzolari approached me to tell me that she'd been offered work with another dental practice in Lockport as their hygiene coordinator. She was going to finally be in a position to advance her career at a larger practice, and I trusted she was telling me the truth. I don't like change any more than the next guy, but I wished her all the best, and that was that.

Apparently, during the previous few months, she'd been telling her patients she was leaving and urging them to follow her. She likely had been telling them, "If you want another appointment with me, you're going to have to make that appointment at a new office opening in the fall." And immediately after that office opened, I started receiving lots of messages from patients informing me they were leaving me. This was no trivial number, either. A steady stream of patients began departing my practice, and it didn't take a rocket scientist to figure out where they were going.

Too late, I remembered I had made the mistake of being honest with my associate one evening, telling her the reason our hygienists were so important. Most patients should only need two cleanings per year, and once a patient was comfortable with a particular hygienist, they would generally stick with them, despite which dentist they worked for. Wendy Fazzolari was now working for my former associate and it was extremely telling how all of this went down. It wasn't due to a bright young doctor leaving. It was only Wendy's patients who left the practice and not those from the other Newfane Family Dentistry hygienists.

It was pretty obvious to me the friendship I thought was so strong was soon going to be irreparable. And, as much as I thought of her husband as a brother, I could no longer treat him that way, and my ability to confide in him as we had in the past was now unfortunately over.

I had just lost another best friend.

CHAPTER THIRTEEN

THE STING

"It takes two to bribe."

- Ljupka Cvetanova

That same year, in late summer 2005, I was making improvements to the new house I bought after my divorce a few years earlier. For the concrete work, I thought of Wendy's husband, Tony. Though he and I rarely talked anymore due to Wendy's inglorious departure, we were once friends, and he had done some great work on the dental office back in the day.

So I approached him and said, "Listen, Tony, you guys still have a dental bill with me, and I need you to take care of it. What do you think about doing some concrete work on my house to pay it off?"

The bill I was referring to was the $1,500 owed for the braces I had made for Tony and Wendy's niece. When Wendy left the practice, I looked into the payments she had made toward those braces, and, low and behold, she hadn't made a single one. Tony seemed open to the idea, so he came by my house, and we chatted.

In the course of our conversation, he said, "Hey Doc, is there any way you can do a root canal on me? I need to show I had a root canal done on tooth 19."

"What are you talking about?" I said. "Need to show?"

"Well," he said, "I have submitted something to my union about having a root canal, and it sounds like they're looking into it, so I need to get a root canal."

"I've never heard of anybody wanting a root canal," I said. "But if you took money from the union for a root canal, and since you have not had that root canal completed, at least not by me, I suggest you pay the money back."

At that, Tony began to explain he had submitted something to the union for $6,970.

"Oh my God, Tony," I said. "If you took money from your union for work that wasn't done, you could get into trouble. I would strongly advise you to pay it back."

"Well," he said, "I don't know what's going to happen with it, but I was hoping you would just do something so this would go through."

Feeling on my guard, I replied, "Tony, I'm not going to do anything just for the sake of putting it through. You need to clear up what you've done, simple as that. If money is the issue, the concrete job for my home should cover you. It's a huge job."

I was building a large, stamped patio in my backyard, with a lot of work involved. "That will give you enough money to do whatever you need to do," I said. "Just make sure you're straight with your union."

To be honest, I was wary that he had approached me with something like this in the first place. I didn't know how the union worked, and I had no intention of helping him break any rules. So I hired him to do my home concrete work and paid him in full so there would be no assumption of aid on my part. It was a $13,000 job, and I paid him by check after he had completed the work. (I still have the receipt.)

A few weeks later, on a Thursday evening, I was having a meeting at home with my consultant, Kristie, who flew in from California to help me train my staff. She worked for a company that helped dental offices with their accountability, to include both doctors and their staff, and she was in town to help with suggestions on how to make my office run more efficiently. We were troubleshooting everything from branding to technology, plus making sure I was coding correctly for every procedure. There's a ton of paperwork and protocols that have to be followed to run an efficient practice, and codes change often with updated explanations, so an outside dental consulting firm can be invaluable.

I was investing a lot of extra money to make sure I had everything working correctly at my office, and Kristie was a second pair of eyes to make absolutely certain we were doing everything by the book. I had just lost a dentist and Wendy, so I was kind of starting anew and wanted to make sure my office was legit, with nothing left to chance. After all, I planned on being there for another 30 years.

Suddenly, there was a knock at my back door. It was Tony. He'd already finished the patio job, and I'd already paid him for all the work he'd done, so I politely excused myself from my meeting for a few minutes. "Sorry, Kristie, let me find out what's up with Tony here, and I'll be back as soon as I've spoken to him. It should only take a few minutes."

I stepped outside with Tony, and we stood in the backyard on top of the new concrete patio. That's when he handed me a bill of sorts and started up again.

"Hey Doc," he said, "are you sure there's nothing else

you can do to help me out with this bill?"

I couldn't believe what I was hearing. "Tony," I said, "please tell me you have paid back the money."

Tony shook his head and begged me again to do the root canal work for him, and then he said, "If we get into trouble over this, there's a lot of people that could lose a lot, you know?"

Was that a threat?

I was surprised to hear this, as I couldn't have made myself any clearer before he started the concrete job. I told him one last time, "Tony, please listen to me. You must pay the money back. I paid you more than you need. I've done everything I can to help you out. There's nothing else I can do. And, by the way, you still need to pay my office for your niece's braces. Just do what's right, okay?"

He replied, "Wendy's supposed to pay that office bill, not me. That's her debt."

The bill Tony gave me was printed on my old company letterhead—Newfane Family Dentistry at 2733 Main Street, the old office—and was dated 2001. This is exactly what the Fazzolaris submitted to their union:

NEWFANE FAMILY DENTISTRY

JAMES E. HOPPE, D.D.S.
SCOTT D. GEISE, D.D.S.

2733 Main St., P.O. Box 38
Newfane, New York 14108
Telephone: (716) 778-7449

Re: Tony Fazzolari Treatment 2001

Emergency Exam	75.00
#19 Root Canal	585.00
#19 Post and Core	275.00
Periodontal Scaling per Quad	
UL	165.00
UR	165.00
LL	165.00
LR	165.00
#31 Periodontal Abcess Irrigation	75.00
Pre Treatment Records	201.00
Comp Treatment Adult Dentition	3099.00
Periodontal Flap Surgery LL	675.00
Periodontal Flap Surgery UL	675.00
#19 Full Coverage Crown	650.00
Total:	**6770.00**

Exhibit A

(The Government presented this document as Exhibit A)

That was the last time I ever talked to Tony.

Then I walked back in through my kitchen door, holding the actual bill Tony had given me. My consultant was still waiting at the kitchen table to resume our meeting and could see that I was concerned about the paper I was now holding in my hand. She asked if everything was okay. I told her what had just happened and voiced my concern that he may have threatened me.

I asked her advice because by now I was starting to worry about my own very limited role in all this. I said, "Could I get into any trouble over this, do you think?"

She replied, "Based on what you've just told me, I can't see how you can be implicated in this at all, but maybe, just to be safe, you should talk to your lawyer."

The important thing about that conversation was I showed her the "bill" that Tony had given me, so she could corroborate that this was the first time I had seen it. I had left the house empty-handed and came back with the bill and spoke to her about it. I certainly had not submitted it to their union, which is what Tony and Wendy would eventually claim.

Later I learned the full story, which tied in with what Tony had told me. Back in 2002, he had submitted this same bill to the union to reimburse him from his health fund. Though he had never undergone a root canal or paid for one or had any other work completed on this fake bill, the union had reimbursed him for the full amount. At the time, that was how I thought it had all gone down.

Probably no one would have been any the wiser if it hadn't been for the disagreement Tony's wife had with his sister, Gina. I don't know the precise circumstances, and I can only imagine the argument Gina and Wendy had, especially with Wendy boasting about how clever she was. Gina had probably heard more than enough from her demeaning sister-in-law and finally cracked, calling the FBI in 2005 to inform them that her brother Tony and his wife Wendy had defrauded the union health fund by submitting false bills. Gina was the same woman whose daughter's braces I had provided, and that was the same balance Wendy still had not paid for.

To look at things from another angle - if that really was the bill that had been submitted, it should never have been paid; it wasn't even close to resembling what any organization would consider a bill of services. It was just a list of treatments, maybe a wish list of the things Tony might need, but with none of the precise codes and other technical and administrative information that must be on a bill. There weren't even any dates of service on it or even a dollar sign. It certainly wasn't something I would or even could have issued because it was as far away from being a bill as a counterfeit $100 bill would be if it was made from construction paper and crayons.

On the advice of my dental consultant, I phoned my corporate attorney, Johnny, and set up a meeting. I immediately brought him up to speed, hoping he would brush away my concerns. Instead, he stayed quiet as he thought for a moment, before saying, "Leave it with me, Scott. I'll make a few phone calls to see if I can figure out what you should do to protect yourself, just to make sure it doesn't come back on you."

"Great," I replied, "Let me know what you come up with, and we can take it from there."

Now, I'm not sure whether Johnny had been approached by the FBI at this point or not, but I'm certain that, on February 17, 2006, a meeting with the FBI was arranged for my attorney and me.

The FBI assured us I was not a target of the investigation; they wanted me simply to verify chart entries and treatments. Johnny told me there was no need for any other representation at that meeting, such as a criminal defense attorney, and that I could explain to them anything I knew about Tony and Wendy Fazzolari. He couldn't have been more wrong.

The meeting took place in Lockport, on the second floor of an old Victorian-looking building. I arrived early and sat chatting with Johnny in his ground floor office as we waited for the FBI to arrive. He wanted to prep me, to give me a rough idea of the sort of ground that would be covered in the meeting and the sort of questions I could expect to be asked. He again made a point of saying, "Listen, you know, Doc, you're not a target of this whole thing. They just want to confirm whether or not Tony had this treatment."

I had brought along the dental records for Tony and Wendy because I was told the FBI wanted to see proof of any work done. Technically, I worried by doing so that I had broken the law since those confidential records are supposed to stay in my office. But they had been requested by the FBI, so I figured it was okay. I planned to settle the matter there and then by showing the FBI the work had not been done because, if it had, it would have appeared in the records.

Then the FBI agents arrived—three men in dark grey suits. I didn't recognize the first two, but the third I recognized as a patient of Wendy's, an agent we will just refer to as MM, although I didn't make the connection at the time.

We all walked up a narrow flight of stairs and into a private meeting room on the second floor. We sat at a huge conference table, which nearly filled the otherwise empty room. Johnny sat with me on one side of the table, two FBI guys took either end, and the other one sat across from us. They introduced themselves and showed me their credentials. They were very polite at first. They explained they were trying to establish whether any treatment had been rendered for a particular bill that had been submitted to Local Union 91 and had been settled.

They showed me the bill—it was a copy of the one Tony had handed to me on that Thursday fall evening several months ago. As I stated before, to anyone in the know, it didn't even come close to resembling a bill. For a claim to be submitted to an insurance company, it has to be perfect, or they will send it back and point out the mistakes. There are so many things that need to be included to successfully submit to an insurance company and get them to pay for services. Even when the paperwork is perfect, it's still a nightmare sometimes to get them to pay, and this piece of paper had none of the critical things needed for that to happen.

There was no treatment coding, no dates of service, and no signature to confirm the work was completed. Despite this, someone at the union had paid it. They shouldn't have. Under normal circumstances, they should have laughed and rejected it, not 99 times out of 100—but every time. There was no credible reason for that bill to have been authorized, other than someone at the union not doing their job properly. This begs the logical question: was this incompetence or collusion?

I'm jumping ahead though because none of this had anything to do with me at this point. I intended to show the FBI I had no involvement or connection with this sorry excuse for a bill. And that would be the end of it.

The agents asked me, "Were any of the treatments listed on this bill ever performed on Tony Fazzolari?"

"No," I replied, unequivocally, "None of this work was ever done for Tony Fazzolari. And just to be clear, this piece of paper cannot be used for a bill."

"Well, who do you think submitted this bill to the union?"

"I wasn't there when this piece of paper was submitted, but I would imagine that Tony, as a union member, would have submitted it himself."

"Who do you think made up the bill?"

"I would ask the Fazzolaris. They're the ones who must have submitted it, so ask them. And once again, just to be clear, *this could never be used as a bill*. So, whoever paid them, if they paid them, probably didn't know what they were doing. And this piece of paper could never be used as a bill for anything I've ever seen in my entire life."

"Well, Dr. Geise, is it possible Wendy could have made the bill for Tony?"

"I have no idea. Ask them. Ask the Fazzolaris. I don't know who made the bill."

"Doc, are you sure you didn't perform any of this treatment?"

"Absolutely. I didn't do any of this treatment."

"Then who submitted this bill?"

"If you're implying that I submitted this, please let me explain to you, one more time, that there are certain things that need to be on a bill for it to even be considered. This is a list of treatments, not a bill, and I've never stepped foot in the union. I don't even know where it is. No, I didn't submit this!"

"Are you familiar with these treatments?"

"I'm familiar with all of them."

"Can you perform them?"

"Yes, of course, I can perform them. I can perform all of these procedures. We do them all the time."

"I see. And have you brought the records for Mr. M?"

"Who?"

"Mr. M. He and his family are also your patients?"

"Yes, but—"

"Do you have their records?"

"Well, no, not with me. They're back in the office. I wasn't asked to bring those."

Rob M was a good friend of Tony's. He also happened to be the head of the Local 91 Union, but I didn't know this at the time.

"Did you ever do any dental work for Mr. M?"

"Nothing, other than cleanings, but I did do some work for his two young boys."

As soon as I mentioned this, the agents pushed a ledger across the table. It was an old-fashioned handwritten ledger that showed I had charged Rob M $700 for orthodontics for his son but had then credited $700 back to them. They leaned back and stared at me in triumph as if they had just caught me in their trap.

"That's a credit adjustment," I explained. I was finding it hard to stay calm. These guys were so pig-headed.

"What's it doing there?"

"I put braces on his son, but he kept knocking the brackets off, so instead of wasting my time putting them back on three times a week, I removed all the brackets and gave Mr. M his money back and simply referred him to an orthodontist. Any return of money goes in my ledger as a credit adjustment."

At this point, Newfane Family Dentistry hadn't switched over fully to computerized accounts, so we were still using the old-fashioned ledger system. The big question was, where had the FBI gotten it from?

"We'll need to see your records for Mr. M to verify the treatments you performed."

"Sure, I have no problem with that. They're in my office. I'm heading there right after this meeting anyway, so I can make a copy and give it to you there. Is that okay? Am I allowed to do that?"

Johnny nodded.

So we agreed to meet at my office in Newfane, about eight miles away. As the agents stood up, I approached the agent to my left and said, "Where do I know you from?" With a very snide look on his face and turning his head toward the other agents with a half-smile, he said, "Jeez, Doc, I used to be a patient of yours."

With that, the three FBI guys left the building and drove off with an unnecessary screech of tires. It was about a 10-minute drive to my office, and I had barely made it into my car when my mobile phone rang. It was Sandy, one of the office cleaning staff.

"Dr. Geise. There are three men here, and they want to come into the office. I've told them you're not here, but they won't go away. I don't know who they think they are, but I'm not letting them in. One of them just called Sherry 'one stupid fucking bitch' . . . right in front of her daughter. They said they're from the FBI."

"The FBI? Jesus, I've just met with them. They know I'm coming down now. We agreed to meet at my office. Couldn't they wait? Where are they now?"

"They're standing outside in the parking lot, talking."

"Okay, well, I'll be there as fast as I can. I'm on my way now." I changed gears, and my engine roared as I floored the accelerator.

When I arrived at the office, the FBI agents were

already gone. They never came back to my office again. I couldn't believe what had just happened. They had attempted to enter my office without permission and presumably intended to look at my files, without a search warrant in the absence of me and my lawyer. When they didn't get their way, they resorted to verbally abusing and bullying my staff.

I was obviously willing to cooperate and give them whatever information they wanted, so why drive at excessive speed to Newfane to get there before me and attempt to enter illegally, or at least hope anyone there would let them in without my permission? If they had a legitimate case, these scare tactics ought to have been totally unnecessary. Was this how things were going to be?

What I didn't know then, but would soon learn, was that the investigation would be predicated on intimidation and bullying and that those same tactics were commonplace.

I phoned Johnny, who then advised me it was time to hire a criminal attorney. He told me to give him a couple of days to make some more phone calls, after which he recommended a criminal attorney from Buffalo called Joel Daniels, adding, "I'll never trust the government again!"

Until then, my business continued to leak patient files to my former associate's office, which was highlighted by an incident that occurred around the same time as my first FBI interview. My other veteran hygienist, the same one who had participated in the gossip chats, decided to shock me in her own way. Julie was now the head of my hygiene department and I had just spoken to her about giving her a pay raise because I didn't want to lose her as well.

Just a few days later, Julie very unexpectedly handed in her notice, not in the usual way, by writing a letter of resignation, or talking with me; she simply walked out and never came back, leaving her keys in an envelope taped to the back entrance. She never returned my calls either because she too had just been hired up the street.

It wasn't long before I hired yet another hygienist, but my business had taken another huge hit, and Julie had taken another tranche of clients with her. I have to believe Wendy convinced her to follow in her footsteps and join her. And I hold my former associate fully accountable for the recruitment of my staff. What a great way to jump-start your own practice! Solicit two hygienists to bring a full schedule of hygiene from another dentist up the street. Business may be business, but why wreck an incredible relationship over money? I had now lost all respect for a doctor I had trusted so dearly.

Now, for the first time, I started to feel anxious. I didn't know who I could trust anymore, especially the government, which was undoubtedly trying to come after me for something. I was just a small-town dentist, absolutely not political in any way, and I certainly never gave them any reason to come after me.

The article entitled *Pride Blooming in Newfane*, written by Teresa Sharp in the Buffalo News, on February 19th, 2006, accurately describes the positive impact my efforts were having in Newfane at that time.

So why on God's earth would they be coming after me?

CHAPTER FOURTEEN

IN THE FRAME

"Recognize that the legal adversarial system is a flawed way to find the truth."

-    Francis P. Karam

I had my first meeting with my newly hired criminal attorney, Mr. Joel L. Daniels, a skeletal man with white wavy hair that framed his deeply lined face. He was wearing an expensive-looking grey suit, a deep purple tie, and an even more expensive double-breasted overcoat.

I knew he had an impressive reputation. In fact, the year after I hired him, he was awarded the peer designation of Super Lawyer, a status conferred on only a select number of expert attorneys in each state. But this was all new to me. I had never even met a criminal attorney before.

I imagined he probably assumed, on the balance of probability and present circumstances, that I was a criminal. Did a defense attorney have to believe in their client's innocence to accept a case? No, surely not—they were ethically bound to represent all clients, including those they believed would be found guilty, as well as those they believed were factually innocent.

Was that it? I was pondering all this as I shook his hand firmly and looked him squarely in the eye as if to convey my innocence and strong moral character. He'd probably experienced hundreds of similarly earnest introductions.

I knew this was a man of action, so we got right down to business. We spoke a little bit about my dental practice, and then one of the first things Mr. Daniels asked was if I knew anything about what the government might have on me.

"I was kind of hoping you'd listen to my side of the story first," I replied.

I immediately felt like I'd been put under the spotlight. I'm sure I was caught up in the emotions of being accused, but it's such an unsettling feeling when being questioned about your own integrity. Did I have to convince my own attorney of my innocence?

"I don't have any priors, maybe a speeding ticket or two, that's it! I haven't done anything wrong. I don't think I've ever even gotten a parking ticket."

"Well, they appear to have *something* because they're looking into you now."

"For what? How do I have any relationship to the union whatsoever, apart from having one or two patients who happen to be union members?"

"It sounds like they're looking into a credit adjustment."

"A credit adjustment just means we gave money back to somebody. If it's an insurance company, and they overpaid us, we also have to do a credit adjustment. Or if a patient paid for something my office was unable to complete, we give money back. A credit adjustment is simply a way to wipe out the charges so the ledger doesn't show an outstanding balance to the patient. So, one way or another, it's giving money back. I explained all of that to the FBI."

"Well, it sounds like they have something with this Mr. M. Did you do a credit adjustment for him? That's what they're looking into."

"Yes, I explained to them I did a credit adjustment because I gave him back $700 for his kid's braces because I removed them. For some reason, they're all over that. I don't know why."

"Well, Mr. M just happens to be the new president of the union. Were you aware of that?"

"Well, I am now. He's the president of the local 91?"

"Yep, plus there's a couple of other things they're looking at—Tony Fazzolari's bill."

"It isn't a bill. It can't be a bill. Please don't refer to it as one."

How many times did I have to repeat this? In meticulous detail, I explained to my criminal attorney— just as I had so patently failed to convince the FBI—that this did not resemble any bill I had ever issued or worked with, and it should never have been paid.

"Well, did you help them prepare this thing?"

"Help them prepare *what*? I only spoke to Wendy about some of the dental work that Tony would need in the future, and I may even have written a few things down for her, but that has nothing to do with a bill. My office never submitted anything. I told the FBI I didn't do the work, and that should be the end of it."

I could sense this guy wasn't getting it, either. Why was it so difficult for people to understand?

"You know, Scott, once the FBI get their claws into you, they never let go, so it might be worth speaking with them at this early stage to see if we can cut some sort of deal."

"A deal? What are you talking about?"

Now it was becoming difficult to disguise my exasperation. Whose side was my attorney on, anyway? I wasn't paying him a ridiculous retainer to reach a deal so soon. This was our first meeting, and it was already starting to dawn on me that this guy might be the wrong fit for me. I was innocent.

Everyone could see the Fazzolaris received money from the union, not me. They had submitted the "bill," not me. Instead of taking responsibility for their own actions, they pinned their crime on someone else. What kind of people were they? And what possible reason could I have had to help them steal, especially when I received absolutely nothing in return?

Daniels was an excellent plea bargain lawyer, an expert at making deals and reducing the prison sentences of guilty people, but he must be able to defend an innocent client as well, or so I had hoped. He had made his name by arranging plea deals for some of the Union 91 guys who had been prosecuted for very serious crimes, and I imagine that they were willing to pay him a lot of money to get off with a reduced sentence.

He was the plea guy for sure: the plea guy for a guilty person. But was he capable of defending an innocent client in a federal court trial? He certainly had a poor bedside manner. He wasn't easy to talk to, and he just didn't seem to understand the dental side of things, the details that clearly exonerated me. Was he even interested in hearing my side of the story?

By the summer of 2006, I decided to bring in another lawyer. I wanted someone closer to home, someone I knew from Lockport, and this fellow had come highly recommended by one of my cousins, who happened to be a paralegal. So I set up a meeting with Mr. Daniels and George Muscato in Muscato's Lockport office.

The most pressing matter was to find out what evidence the FBI thought they had against me, and it all came back to the "bill." The Fazzolaris were insisting I issued the bill in return for Tony doing my concrete for free. This just didn't make any sense because, as I had explained to my two attorneys, "I have the receipts which prove I paid him money for the concrete. So what would be my incentive for giving them a fake bill in return for nothing?"

Muscato replied, "It sounds like they're going after you because the bill was instrumental in getting the money paid by the union."

"Well then," I replied. "Let's go speak to the union. Let's find out who submitted the bill and who gave them the money. One way or another, whoever paid them must have known this wasn't a bill. They have to have known there was nothing on there to show I verified the work was done."

I then told them that the year before (2005), I had discovered someone from the union had called my office to verify whether the Fazzolari treatment had been done or not—I wasn't there at the time and had no knowledge of the call—but it seems as if someone in my office told them the work had been done. Clearly, that someone had to have been Wendy Fazzolari.

That certainly explained why the FBI was so fixated on the bill. They knew somebody had lied. Either it was the person from my office who verified that the work had been done, or it was me for insisting the work had never been done.

Contacting the union got us nowhere. We just went around in circles, and no matter what facts we tried to convey to those people, they appeared to fall on deaf ears. It made no sense that I would insist the work hadn't been done if that implicated me in fraud. Surely if I had indeed forged the "bill" (regardless of whether or not it was in return for concrete work), I would be insisting I *had* completed the work.

Everyone seemed to have made up their minds that I was lying, or at least, that I was the guy who was going to take the rap because other parties such as the Fazzolaris had already made a deal with the FBI. A simple X-ray of Tony's teeth would have settled the matter conclusively, but these FBI agents didn't seem to be interested in the truth. That's not how it worked. Someone wanted to target me so the focus could be taken off someone else.

As the months passed, we went over the same old ground, until toward the end of 2006, I was shocked to discover a US Attorney was now involved in my case. Three weeks before Christmas, Daniels phoned me with more scary news.

"The government isn't quite sure if they're going to indict you yet, but they're seriously thinking about it."

"For what?" I vented. "How can they possibly indict me?"

I knew that, once indicted, I would be screwed. First of all, my reputation would be destroyed. Warren Buffett, the oracle from Omaha, has preached this his entire life: "You can afford to lose money, but you can't afford to lose your reputation." I was a local guy who'd never been in trouble, but an indictment has guilt written all over it. And, as soon as the indictment became public, my fate would be sealed.

At that point, it wouldn't really matter if I was innocent or not. All the media wanted was to create a story about a doctor who must have done something he shouldn't have. And if the federal government was taking the time to pursue this small town man, he must've done something *really* bad.

I gathered my thoughts for a moment and then said, "There's no way we can allow this to go any further. I don't want an indictment, no matter what."

"Well," Daniels said, "we have a couple of choices. We either start thinking long term about trying to mitigate risk, or we allow the government more time."

"Allow them more time?" I yelled, "I haven't even spoken to them for 10 months, during which time we've been banging our heads against a brick wall not knowing what they're after. If they don't have anything now, why should that change?"

"We certainly don't want an indictment to come out just before Christmas," said Daniels.

"Mr. Daniels, we don't want an indictment at any time. I haven't done anything wrong—"

"Doc, please, call me Joel."

"No sir, not until you get me out of this. Until you do, you are Mr. Daniels. With all due respect, I'm not going to be all buddy-buddy until all of this is over. We need to take care of this. It needs to be over with as soon as possible."

"I don't think they have anything. You know they don't have anything, so let's just give them a bit of extra time," Mr. Daniels said.

That's when he not only threw me a curveball, but he did it so abruptly that, if this wasn't a metaphor, he'd have dislocated his shoulder.

"I need you to sign something. I'll post it to you."

"What is it?"

"It's a waiver."

"A waiver? For what?"

"Well, the five-year statute of limitations will soon run out on the Fazzolari bill, which is a key piece of evidence. It was submitted in 2002, so the FBI needs to indict someone soon or it'll become inadmissible. However, if you sign a waiver, giving them extra time to investigate you without having to rush, they have agreed not to indict you before Christmas."

"So, let me get this straight," I replied slowly. I took a couple of deep breaths to try and control my rising rage. "If I, an innocent man, who has been the main focus of an FBI investigation for the better part of a year, based on a key piece of evidence with which I have no connection whatsoever, waive my right for that flimsy evidence to become inadmissible, in return for my cooperation, the FBI agrees to wait until after Christmas before destroying my life?"

I looked at Mr. Daniels with contempt, then said, "Besides, assembling a grand jury over the Christmas holiday will be practically impossible, so why don't we just let the statute of limitations run out? Then they'll have to drop the case."

As the wizened, presumably cynical attorney, he fired back, "If they can get all of the information, the government will realize they have nothing to pursue. But, if they indict, then your reputation in Newfane will be hit hard. If you sign the waiver, they'll have the time to go through everything."

"What *everything*? What more could there possibly be? They've already done nothing for a year!"

"Well, let's just give them the benefit of the doubt. They'll find they have nothing and soon it'll be over."

So, like a fool, I trusted my lawyer, and signed the waiver.

Christmas came and went. Then another six months came and went, during which time there was zero contact from the FBI. I went back to work, tried to put it out of my mind, and continued to concentrate on my boys and their schedules. Even so, I kept phoning Mr. Daniels to ask him if there was any news. The answer was always the same. No news. No news. On and on it went, month after month.

All I received were some grand jury subpoenas demanding treatment records and invoices for a handful of other patients, which I dutifully supplied since everything otherwise was in good order, and I had nothing to hide. But as the end of each month arrived, I kicked myself for daring to believe that maybe this would be the month when this nightmare would finally be over.

My youngest son was only three years old when my marriage broke up, and he was only six when the FBI came knocking on my door and my life started falling apart.

When all of this kicked off, if I didn't have the boys, I was doing everything I could to save my practice, my well-being, and ultimately my liberty. But when the boys were staying with me, I tried to forget about all the legal stuff and spend quality time with them as the center of my focus. It was tough compartmentalizing like that. We men are supposed to be experts at dividing our lives, but the reality is extremely difficult. I had no other choice. I couldn't drag the boys into my mental torment, nor could I use it as an excuse not to be fully present for them.

I've always been acutely aware of the importance of having a healthy and positive internal dialogue, by which I mean the conversations we have with ourselves. We live our lives based on a series of conversations we have, not so much with other people, but with ourselves. If you think about it, you've probably already had a couple of chats with yourself today. Think of all the, "Oh, I just don't want to get out of bed today" conversations, the "Oh my God, I can't face this busy day" conversations, and the "I can do this" pep talks and the "I'm not going to let this bother me" self-counseling—these are all part of the everyday activities that govern our lives.

We talk to ourselves constantly throughout the day. Individuals who can control and improve these conversations can truly make a difference in their own lives, and the lives of everyone around them. There have been times during my life when I've struggled to get myself into the right mindset, just to get out of bed in the morning, but no matter what we have to face, that ability to talk oneself back into the game is a crucial skill I had to draw on many, many times.

Finally, in June 2007, I received a phone call from Mr. Daniels. "Doc, we need to meet. Not great news, I'm afraid. The US Attorney is bringing an indictment against you. I've got it in front of me right now. You have nine counts."

"Nine counts?" I said, collapsing into my chair. "This is crazy. How can-- What are they?"

"Well, the first is that you aided and abetted union depositors to steal from their welfare fund."

"What? Are they crazy? What about all the others?"

"The other ones are all treatment related."

"Treatment related? But I've never had a single complaint from a patient, and I've never had an issue with any insurance carrier throughout my entire career. So where's the complaint for treatment, and how can the FBI pull these?"

"Well, they've got eight counts stemming from treatment that was never done, or allegedly never done."

"Who's claiming I never did their work?" I paused, then said, "They must be getting these lies from Wendy, who I'm sure would say anything to save her own ass."

"Well, it looks like they found this information from the records they subpoenaed."

"Are you—are they saying they have proof I submitted false insurance bills to insurance companies for treatment I never did? And they figured this out by only looking at the notes in my patients' records? Is that what you're saying?"

"That's exactly what they're saying. For eight different patients."

"Well, where did that information come from?"

There were no recent complaints from insurance companies or patients, and I certainly had never billed for treatment on patients I didn't perform.

"Ah, well let me tell you something. Our government could indict a ham sandwich if it wanted to."

I might know that now, but I didn't know it at this time.

"The billing information was presented to the grand jury," Mr. Daniels said, "but we can't be at the grand jury. That's something they produced to get the indictment."

"So now what?" I asked.

"So, you haven't been arrested."

"I know that," I said, stating the obvious.

"There will now be an arraignment, which will take place on July 3, where you present yourself before the judge. So, you've got less than a month to make a really important decision. Do you want to look toward a plea to get out of this thing, or do you want to plead not guilty?"

"Let me tell you what I want you to do. I want you to take this indictment and go shove it up that prosecutor's ass. I'm not guilty, and I'm going to fight this to the end. If they say they've got shit on me, then you guys need to find out exactly what they think they have. We're going to fight this thing, dammit, tooth and nail."

The Fazzolaris and the FBI had turned my world upside down. The selfish, immoral lies of a couple who were sold out by their own family members had now led to the complete destruction of an innocent man, his career, and his integrity.

"Okay, but some advance warning here, Doc. Once we get to that arraignment, you're going to be headline news. You want to prepare yourself for that. Newfane is a small town, and you're going to be a big story for a while. If you've got friends and family you need to talk to, you'd better do it now."

CHAPTER FIFTEEN

ARRAIGNMENT

"I can tell you one thing: you are quickly going to find out who your true friends are."

- Shirley Geise

At an arraignment, the accused is informed of the charges brought against him and is allowed to either plead guilty, if he admits that he has committed the crime charged, or plead not guilty if he denies it and/or wants to exercise his right to put the government to the test – of proving beyond a reasonable doubt that he is guilty on the crimes charged.

On Tuesday, July 3, 2007, I drove to Buffalo with my parents. We met up with my legal counsel, Daniels and Muscato, on the ground floor of the old, decrepit Statler building, and then we all walked together over to the federal courthouse, where I was about to be arraigned.

As we arrived inside, we first had to negotiate the usual security checkpoint. As I stood in line, watching my parents place their valuables into a tray, I could see the news media set up already to film our procession into the elevator.

Daniels advised us to walk normally and refrain from hiding our faces from the camera. If you've never been in this situation, count your lucky stars. I tried to place myself into my parents' shoes that day, and I can't imagine what was going through their heads. If my child were placed in the same predicament, my heart would be utterly broken.

When we all piled into the elevator, it seemed to take forever for the doors to slide shut, and, all the while, the ghastly news cameras were flashing. We rose to the fifth floor, and it was at that point that Daniels informed us we would only be seeing a magistrate, not the federal judge to which we'd been assigned, the Honorable Richard J. Arcara.

I had received conflicting reports about Judge Arcara from various people in the know, so I was a little confused as to why a magistrate would be overseeing the initial arraignment today. I'd never been through this before, so I had no other choice but to rely upon the experience of my defense counsel.

Once in the courtroom, my family and I sat together on one of the benches. My two lawyers proceeded through the waist-high swinging door and took their place at the table for the accused. The government's attorneys, along with their trusty FBI investigators, paraded in just a few moments before the magistrate. At the All Rise signal, my counsel motioned for me to stand up, and then we all sat back down.

Magistrate Scott was a very soft-spoken black judge. His voice was calming, so when he began the proceedings, I couldn't help but feel as though my good name would eventually be vindicated—that all I had to do was put my faith in the integrity of the system and go through the actions needed to prove my innocence.

After all the charges had been read, Magistrate Scott

asked me to stand. I could hear him talking, but all the while I had the surreal feeling of dissociation - *this wasn't really happening to me.* The last four words I'd heard him say were, "How do you plead?"

I didn't hesitate, naively thinking my haste was an intrinsic and obvious signifier of my innocence: "NOT GUILTY to all counts, Your Honor."

I cringed when the counts were read, and blushed, and felt ashamed—all at once.

The first count stated, "Between on or about December 2001 and January 9, 2002, the exact dates being unknown to the Grand Jury, in the Western District of New York, the defendant, SCOTT D. GEISE, did knowingly, willfully, and unlawfully aid and abet another person whose identity is known to the grand jury to embezzle, steal, and abstract and convert to such other person's own use in the approximate amount of $6,970.00, the money, funds, securities, premiums, credits, property, and other assets of Laborers International Union of North America, Local 91, Welfare Fund Personal Account Program, an employee welfare benefit plan, subject to Title I of the Employee Retirement Income Security Act of 1974, all in violation of Title 18, United States Code, Sections 664 and 2."

Counts 2–9 stated, "On or about the dates listed, in the Western District of New York and elsewhere, in a matter involving a health-care benefit program as defined by Title 18, United States Code, Section 24(b), the defendant, SCOTT D. GEISE, did knowingly and willfully make, and cause to be made, materially false, fictitious, and fraudulent statements and representations in connection with the delivery of and payment for healthcare benefits and services by Newfane Family Dentistry, P.C., in that the defendant submitted, and caused to be submitted, false, fictitious, and fraudulent dental insurance claims in connection with health-care benefit programs, in which the defendant sought payment for dental services which the defendant knew had not been actually provided to patients by the defendant or Newfane Family Dentistry, P.C."

Generally, the charges included the initials of eight separate patients, service dates ranging from September 2002 to November 2006, as well as, in each case, a claim of $350 for a fraudulent billed "occlusal guard," for a grand total of $2,800 (less than for a case in Small Claims court—and here it was, a federal case).

In fact, I had manufactured eight customized occlusal guards for those eight individual patients and then gave them the bleach *for free,* which they could add to the guard to get free teeth whitening. I had given each patient a free bleach kit to use with the guard each night—kind of an incentive to start wearing the guard and get more comfortable with it.

The FBI decided I had committed a crime because they claimed I hadn't manufactured the guards at all. Insurance companies are very particular that they will not reimburse for bleach kits because so many people wanted them in the early 2000s, but each person was eligible for one occlusal guard during the lifetime of his or her coverage.

My patients received the benefit of both, for the exact same price as the occlusal guard on its own, but the prosecutor pushed it as fraud because of the bleach kits. At the time, neither my patients nor the insurance company had a problem with this arrangement.

Furthermore, if it was argued I possessed an intent to defraud, that would be ridiculous. I received no financial benefit, and there were a total of only eight cases over a five-year billing period—it was hardly a criminal empire.

According to the CDT book of coding, an occlusal guard or night guard is something you wear at night to protect your teeth from the grinding forces we place upon our teeth while we sleep. Hence the name. Bruxism is simply the medical term used for grinding teeth. The thicker the tray material, the more cumbersome and difficult it is to wear, so we custom-made our guards to be thinner and easier to wear throughout the night.

A take-home bleach kit is a cosmetic dental appliance that allows a patient to apply bleaching gel to their teeth overnight and can be made out of the exact same material as a night guard. Bleach kits don't have to be worn solely at night, but most patients find that time to be the most convenient. A night guard itself, if the patient already has one, can alternatively be used as a bleach kit by simply adding gel to it overnight.

So we can look at this in two separate ways: Either I make a night guard and put bleach in it if that's what the patient wants, or I make a bleach kit and have the patient continue to use the tray as their occlusal guard or night guard after they're finished bleaching. There really is no difference, and I discussed this issue with my patients every time we made one.

Importantly, it was the patient's decision to bleach, not mine. If the insurance company wanted to deny payment on the night guard, then the patient would not have their benefit, and they would have to fight it out with their own insurance company. Either way, they would still owe me for the service that was provided. In either instance, it was the patient's choice to move forward with treatment.

The arraignment hearing was all over very quickly and my parents and I stumbled outside into the daylight and drove home. Mr. Daniels was right about the newspaper coverage. It was some consolation that a few news reports looked at the wider picture and contextualized my indictment.

There had been a massive ongoing investigation conducted by the US Department of Labor, the FBI, and the IRS into federal racketeering within the leadership of the Local 91. Union members had used extensive violence and threats of violence against contractors, independent workers, and members of other unions to dominate the construction industry in the Niagara County area, as well as commit vandalism against nonunion construction projects.

Unfortunately, the media somehow made me a part of this bigger picture. Apparently, in August 2006, three of the former officials of the Local 91 had pled guilty to racketeering charges and a fourth to extortion. This meant a grand total of 18 union members had been successfully prosecuted over the previous four years. The FBI had been trying to bring some of these people to justice for decades.

Speaking to *the New York Times*, Laurie Bennett, special agent in charge of the Federal Bureau of Investigation's local office, had called it "the most significant FBI criminal investigation in western New York in the past 20 years . . . because of the widespread violence and the significant and devastating economic loss to the community."

Also quoted was Superintendent John R. Chella of the Niagara Falls Police, who said, "It wasn't only the implied threat that you played by the rules of Local 91 or you didn't do business at all, but there have been documented cases of physical violence, damage to property, and intimidation. The message was clearly sent; either play the game or pay the price."

This wasn't just petty thuggery. These people were highly dangerous and violent. One FBI witness, a nonunion worker at an asbestos-removal project, "described how Local 91 pickets threw steel pipes and other objects at him and his coworkers and shouted threats," and, that night, "two bricks with explosives taped to them crashed through windows at the apartment where Mr. S. and three others were sleeping. One landed about a foot from his head, with the explosion causing permanent hearing loss in his right ear and burning his bedding."

One of the Local 91 members indicted by that FBI investigation was none other than the former local president, who had worn a wire for the FBI to help secure convictions for the firebombing and had testified against many of his union colleagues to put them behind bars. Mr. M happened to be a partner in a contracting business with Tony Fazzolari, called Solid Ground Concrete. No wonder the FBI had come sniffing around the credit adjustment I had given him.

It didn't take me long before I was fairly confident I had become embroiled in all of this simply because of plea bargain testimony from both Fazzolari and Mr. M. My attorneys released a statement to the press maintaining my innocence and accusing the Justice

Department of relying on "the word of an admitted union embezzler and cheat," but to marginal effect.

What took me by surprise was the massive outpouring of support I received from my patients and colleagues. My friend, Dr. Ken Kurbs, organized "The Friends of Scott Geise," and proceeded to get letters submitted on my behalf.

By now, my practice was back on its feet. I had a great consulting firm providing guidance, and we were all working efficiently as a team. My new staff took up the slack and went the extra mile during this difficult time. The office was running full steam ahead, and we were even picking up a lot of new patients—many were even returning from my former associate. It was awesome.

Likewise, so many of my patients made a point of verbalizing their support, expressing their dismay at what had happened to me, and wishing me well for a positive outcome. Local 91 had such a bad reputation for being thugs and criminals that I guess my patients knew there was no way I was involved in such hardcore criminal racketeering, but the FBI was certainly pushing it.

Another impetus from the government, which fed into my indictment, was that, in 2005, the government had cracked down on widespread abuses within Medicare and Medicaid. US Attorneys were under a lot of pressure to bring to justice any doctors and dentists involved specifically in Medicare and Medicaid fraud. This was the confluence of forces driving the government and law enforcement agenda. Ironically, I had *never* participated in either of those government insurance programs. Not Medicare and not Medicaid.

After the initial flurry of publicity, things quieted

down, and I started to feel less conspicuous. But as the weeks and months rolled by, I became increasingly anxious about our lack of preparations for what I assumed would be an imminent trial. Unfortunately, my boys (now attending Desales Catholic School) were hearing some comments about their dad's name being in the news and were suffering mean comments from other kids.

I even heard that some prominent people in town were saying they saw me dragged out of my office in handcuffs. I was never arrested, and, throughout this entire legal ordeal, I was never handcuffed and dragged away from anywhere. It's human nature, I guess, for some people to need to feel they're in the know or must exaggerate their knowledge.

That's how gossip starts—and thus the saying, attributed first to Mark Twain, "A lie can travel around the world and back again while the truth is still lacing up its boots."

I kept calling Mr. Daniels to try to get things moving. Weren't we supposed to be going to trial soon? And shouldn't we be preparing to put me on the stand so I could explain precisely what I did or didn't do? I just wanted to get this over with and prove my innocence, but that was the last thing on my attorney's mind.

"Gosh, Doc, I don't think it would be a good idea to put you on the stand. You know, they think you've already incriminated yourself with this bill and um . . ."

"How could I possibly incriminate myself with submitting a bill I didn't submit in the first place and had nothing to do with? They know that the Fazzolaris submitted it!"

"Look, Doc. You have a nine-count indictment. If they

find you guilty on just one count, they're very likely to find you guilty on all nine."

"Well, you know what?" I replied, barely able to contain my frustration. "I thought it was best to fight before things went to trial. Most of these things happen before trial."

"Well, Doc, that's why I was trying to get you to plead out, before we got here."

"Plead out to nothing, take a massive hit, plead out to a felony? Screw that!"

And so it went on. As the weeks passed, I kept asking my attorney when we were going to trial and when we could expect to get any information back from the government about their evidence on me. He explained to me this part of the process was called "discovery," whereby both parties had a legal obligation to exchange information.

"So what does the government have to show us, then? What's in their discovery?"

"Well, we don't know yet because they haven't sent us anything. We're still waiting."

"Can't you demand it? There's not even a trial date set. What are we doing here?"

"Well," replied Mr. Daniels, "we're just going to wait this out for a little longer."

And so we waited some more, and I tried to put as much of it out of my mind as I possibly could.

This was just as well because, at the end of summer, I found myself faced with yet another legal battle.

CHAPTER SIXTEEN

THE SCHOONER

"Land was created to provide a place for boats to visit."
- Brooks Atkinson

The previous year, in 2006, a high school friend approached me to discuss his idea of bringing a historic 80-foot schooner to Olcott Harbor. I was also interested in doing anything I could to foster much-needed tourism in Olcott, so I decided to assist in the project.

I told my friend, "I don't care if I ever make a dime out of this project, but I don't want to lose my shirt on it either." Keith set up the business plan, and we figured out all the details needed to make Olcott a summer attraction again. We checked out boats along the New England coast and finally found the ship that would create an immediate impact on Lake Ontario.

So we sailed a historic boat down from Maine and began the business of running excursions for up to 30 people at a time. She spent a very promising first summer moored in Olcott Harbor.

The harbor town of Olcott had been a huge attraction back in the early 1900s, but not much was happening there anymore.

(The schooner entering Olcott Harbor with Toronto in the
distant sunset)

My vessel was a two-post, 80-foot wooden John Alden
Schooner, the kind you simply don't see anymore on Lake
Ontario. During my childhood, I used to see old pictures
of these incredible boats that came over from Toronto and
moored in Olcott's deep marina. It seems like all dreams
have a price to them, but this adventure was already
getting costly. In addition to pouring money into the
schooner, I even invested $13,000 of my own money into
the Town of Newfane dock so the project would be a
success.

But people loved that boat. They came from all around
to book a tour. It was similar to one of those wooden
schooners that used to run during the War of 1812. It was
a piece of living history you could climb aboard. I spent a
lot of money just getting the boat back to Olcott, but if I'd
wanted to make money, I would have invested in the stock

market. I didn't care because it was always about regenerating something magical from my local community's past.

The plan was to sail the boat down the Eastern Coast every fall to avoid the winters on Lake Ontario. The boat would then do tours throughout the winters in St Petersburg, Florida, and then return to Lake Ontario in the late spring. We would sell spots on each leg of the trip heading both north and south, so, in this way, the investment could be recouped.

On the first return from Florida, fate kept us in the Gulf of Mexico for that hurricane season, but excitement for the coming winter was already growing. The Tampa Bay Buccaneers had already expressed interest in having my schooner tethered offshore during their home games, and, being a black-hulled ship, it certainly fit the Buccaneer look.

In October 2007, I had already planned for the boat to winter in St. Petersburg, Florida. My shipwright, George Conway, who was looking after it for me, watched as the boatyard craned the schooner out of the water, ready for its annual inspection. That inspection would be performed by the Coast Guard and would be the perfect time to do all the routine maintenance, such as applying new caulking between the boards—whatever was needed to keep it seaworthy.

Of course, the longer it stayed out of the water in dry dock, the more it cost me in fees. Everything just needed to be signed off by the Coast Guard and then the boat could return to the water. I couldn't be present during this inspection because I was back in Newfane sitting chairside in my dental practice, so I had everything set up ahead of time with Keith and George to ensure an efficient day.

This particular afternoon, I got a phone call from George. There was a problem with the boat. "Doc, you're not going to believe this, but the idiot Coast Guard has damaged the boat."

"What do you mean damaged the boat? How?"

"Well, he's supposed to check to make sure the wood is sound, detect rot, but instead of using his finger, as you would to check the ripeness of a peach, he decided to use a screwdriver and has damaged planks on the boat."

"What? Why didn't you stop him?"

"He waited until your buddy Keith and I left for a cup of coffee. The water was still draining out of the hull, but when I returned, he was underneath the boat, and when I saw what he'd done, I was all over him. Now I'm going to have to replace an entire plank."

"So the Coast Guard damaged it and you can verify that?"

"Absolutely. I'm looking at him nose to nose right now. I'm getting his superior's number, and I'll find out what we have to do to replace the plank. But I'm telling you now, it's going to be tough."

"Why?"

"Well, the planks are all long leaf pine. They harvested this stuff out of South Carolina to make schooners back in the early 1900s."

"So?"

"So, there's no more long leaf pine left."

"Can't you use something else?"

"Absolutely not. You have to use the same wood so that it expands and shrinks in the water at the same rate as all the other planks."

"So, are you telling me you can't repair it?"

"I can't. This dickhead ripped up your garboard plank, the longest damn piece of wood on the entire boat. I don't think we can find the materials to repair this boat."

On top of that, the Coast Guard refused to certify the boat until I had fixed the plank and also refused to accept responsibility for the damage, so I had to hire another law firm in Florida to sort out this mess.

Now I was forced to battle on two fronts with four attorneys, which, as you can imagine, was a considerable financial drain and certainly provided the necessary mental strain to coax me into a plea.

CHAPTER SEVENTEEN

SUPERSEDING INDICTMENT

"The presumption of innocence is now the presumption of guilt. The burden of proof is a travesty because the proof is often lies."

- John Grisham

Still, there was no sign the government lawyers were going to set a trial date, even though the law states they must do so within 70 days of my arraignment. My resolve—to fight in court to prove my innocence—hadn't changed, as the idea of plea bargaining simply wasn't an option. And I was damned sure my attorneys hadn't waived my right to a speedy trial.

By October we were way past the 70 days to trial, and under those circumstances, the government was under a legal obligation to dismiss the case or go to trial without the evidence they needed. Shit or get off the pot, in more vulgar terms.

Instead, they were surgically cutting me, bleeding me to death, and my attorneys were allowing them to do so—the proverbial death by a thousand cuts. Then, in December, my lawyer told me some shocking news: that my "mere" nine-count indictment was going to be replaced by a superseding indictment alleging a staggering 65 counts, adding in more phony treatment claims, as well as five counts of IRS fraud.

Now, the way it's supposed to work is the old indictment is supposed to be dissolved and the new indictment has to be brought before the grand jury. I don't have any proof for this, but I don't think my superseding indictment was properly acquired. I think the prosecutors were so fixated on my pleading out that they failed to follow the correct procedure.

One thing was certain: The charges that were piled on were obviously unrelated to the first charge, so my lawyers were entitled to file a motion for severance to split the superseding indictment into three totally separate groups.

The first group was just Count 1, relating to Tony Fazzolari's "bill."

The second group included Counts 2–58, which were charges of submission of false and fraudulent dental insurance claims.

The third group was new Counts 59–65, which were for filing false income tax returns.

Splitting them would enable me to fight segmented counts, separating the indictment into three separate sets of possible crimes, rather than fending off a scattershot of 65 counts in one trial alone. But, once again, the feds resisted this, and it would take another whole year to achieve a severance and finally fix a first trial date.

Meanwhile, support for me within the Newfane area and the wider community remained buoyant. Even the National Legal and Policy Center raised the possibility of my innocence. An article published on June 30, 2008, by Carl Horowitz, stated, "Geise's attorneys, Joel Daniels and George Muscato, insist their client is innocent. That might well be the case."

The article highlighted that Wendy Fazzolari had access to all the paperwork in the office, implying "that she ran a renegade operation," but it also acknowledged that "the case may hinge on [my] word versus that of an imprisoned former member of the local union, whose goon-squad style of intimidation of contractors and non-union workers has been chronicled frequently in this publication."

But it was certainly tough for the government to go after Wendy Fazzolari, now that they'd already granted her immunity from prosecution. Why did they do that? I believe they did that because she had been their star witness from the very beginning at the Grand Jury and someone who, as I've always surmised, was carefully protected by someone in the agency.

A whole slew of motions followed, setting and postponing hearings and allowing time for discovery and pretrial discussions to be had. Each time one of these motions appeared before the court, the resulting order would read, "Now, it is hereby ORDERED, that the time in this action from and including [9/12/2008], is properly excluded from the time within which the defendant should be brought to trial, in accordance with the Speedy Trial Act, pursuant to Title 18, United States Code Sections 31 61 (h) (8) (A). The Court further finds that as of 9/12/2008, zero days of Speedy Trial Act time will have elapsed in this action and 70 days remain in the period within which defendant must be tried."

So, instead of days slipping away from the government's case, the feds manipulated the system to reset the clock each time a motion was filed, which is contrary to law, and something that has, and continues to be, abused in many other federal cases as well. The clock should tick, or be paused—not reset! I feel for all of those people out there who are having their own constitutional rights abused right now by this carelessness.

I continued to run my successful dentist practice, although I did lose several dozen patients after the charges against me rose from nine to 65. Indeed, it appeared the public's perception of my guilt increased in direct proportion to the number of counts included in my superseding indictment. That's understandable, of course. It's human nature to follow the principle of no smoke without fire.

And the smoke around me had just increased by a factor of seven. However, I kept my focus and continued to treat my patients with the same dedication I always had.

During all this legal activity, I was the head coach of the Newfane boys' lacrosse team. I had brought the new game to town back in 2005, and more and more kids were signing up each year. Even though my financial future was at stake, I couldn't let these kids down. We were starting a new season, and my assistant coach, Bob Krupp, gave me the support and spiritual encouragement to soldier on.

To help make this program a reality, I invested close to $15,000 of my own money, supplying the safest helmets I could for my players and buying jerseys for both the boys' and girls' teams. That generosity in itself should have strengthened my case to the point where someone would say, "This doesn't sound right!" Why would anyone give so much away to their community if they were so selfish and greedy? Or was that illegal too? If I had wanted more money in my own pocket, why would I have given to the community in such a generous way?

The court was still trying to decide whether the counts should be split up into three separate trials, and it seemed like an eternity trying to get something moving. My motion to sever had been countered with equal vigor by the prosecutors, and a hearing was finally set before Judge Arcara for October 31, 2008. There's no better way to spend Halloween than in a federal courthouse fighting for your life. Believe me, nothing could be scarier.

My attorney Mr. Daniels went first, and by the time he was done, it was pretty clear the 65 counts should not have been joined in the first place. After the government countered, Judge Arcara said, "And the government, Mr. Moscati (the government prosecutor at that time), I have absolutely no idea . . . I've read your argument three times, and I still don't understand it. Would you please explain to me why you think this case is distinguishable from those two cases?"

The judge was talking about the *Halper* and *Shellef* cases, which had set the precedent against the government piling on charges of different origins against defendants. As my lawyer had concluded, this was a matter of having to "dodge 65 bullets" at the same time, which was unfair in any legal system where fairness absolutely matters.

Finally, after sitting on it for a few weeks, the judge granted our motion and severed the cases. At that time, the judge did defer to the government, asking which of the three groups of counts it was prepared to prosecute: Count 1, Counts 2–58, or Counts 59–65.

Predictably, the government chose Count 1 because that was the only count out of 65 that was commenced by a formal complaint. The government had always wanted me to plead guilty to Count 1, defrauding the union. All the other counts were piled on to leverage a pretrial plea. The court now set a date for jury selection on May 12, 2009.

So there I was facing a maximum sentence of 122 years in prison, verbally affirmed by the prosecutor in court. Unbelievable! How could they be allowed to pile on so much crap that I could spend multiple lifetimes in prison? In New York, a first-degree murder conviction was only 20–25 years mandatory.

One of the groups of charges involved an insurance company called Delta Dental. On November 11, 2006, the FBI telephonically interviewed an auditor at this company, Christine Danford, who had performed some sort of comparative analysis suggesting I was guilty of some elaborate fraud against the insurance companies. This is how the FBI reported her findings:

"Using license number ******, SCOTT GEISE had billed DELTA DENTAL MI $1,935,861.67 from 2001 to the current billing cycle of 2006. During that same period, GEISE billed 110 times for occlusal guards, at a total cost of approximately $25,000.00. An analysis of the claims received for license number ****** versus claims received from all other New York general practitioners in the DELTA DENTAL MI plan for the year 2005 identified multiple inconsistencies. Some of the inconsistencies identified were that GEISE billed an average of $2,600.00 per patient per year, while his peers billed an average of $580.00; GEISE waited an average of 157 days to submit his claims, while his peers averaged three (3) days; GEISE submitted claims for an average of eight (8) teeth per patient, while his peers submitted claims for an average of one (1) to two (2) teeth per patient; GEISE submitted claims for an average of five (5) minor restorations, such as fillings, per patient, while his peers submitted claims for an average of one (1) per patient; GEISE submitted claims for 100 major restorations, such as crowns, and his primary age group for these procedures was 36 to 49-year-old patients, while his peers submitted claims for an average of 14 major restorations; and GEISE submitted claims for 50 anterior crowns, while his peers submitted an average of 17 claims."

I have no idea where the FBI got this information, but I could prove it was false and would never stand up to scrutiny in a court of law. The FBI themselves only found eight issues of occlusal guards, but this audit produced 110? To further prove these were false allegations, I pulled every single one of those insurance claims from our files to work out for myself what our average claim was per patient. What did I find? That I was submitting for $514 per patient, a few dollars below average, which made sense.

But here's the clincher: insurance companies place a cap on how much can be claimed each year—something the FBI was apparently unaware of. Delta's cap at that time was between $1,200 to $1,500 per year, so it would have been impossible for them to pay me anything more than the cap, certainly not the average of $2,600 per patient per year that the FBI claimed I had received.

Plain and simple, I believe someone, or some group of people, had fabricated this claim to look like something it was not. But it partially explains why they subsequently indicted me for failing to declare some of my income during this same period. When, quite simply, I hadn't earned what they claimed I had.

In March, a revised trial date was set for July 7, 2009, at 9:00 a.m. But before we look at the trial, I'd like to explain how Counts 2 to 9 and Counts 10 to 58— submitting false and fraudulent dental insurance claims— came to be.

Until 2005, my dental practice was no different from many other dental practices across the country. Dentists perform treatments and then submit their fees to the insurance company, which subsequently pays all or part of the cost. It's a very tightly regulated industry, so it's vitally important to code everything correctly and to claim for the correct materials and procedures. However, there are some areas where a discrepancy arises between the work done and the fees the insurance companies are willing to pay. One of those areas involves composite fillings.

Before 2005, whenever I supplied a patient with a composite filling, I would submit an insurance claim for a composite filling. However, many insurance companies, even to this day, do not cover composite fillings and will only pay for the old amalgam fillings, which are less expensive. I was well used to receiving letters back from insurance companies, rejecting my claim for payment of a composite filling (which is a white-colored filling), but paying me instead for the cheaper amalgam (a silver filling).

I would get paid to supply an amalgam filling but would actually supply a superior and more expensive composite filling and take a hit on the shortfall. In other words, I didn't charge the patient or the insurance company for the extra cost. My business—like thousands of other dental practices nationwide who billed the same way—would absorb the loss to provide better patient care.

When the FBI examined these transactions, they rushed to judge my billings as fraudulent, even though the insurance company and the patient fully understood the circumstances. I had never received any complaints from insurance companies or patients, and all was above board. So where was my intent to defraud anyone? Where was my financial gain? I have always been open and honest about the actual work I have performed.

Billing insurance companies in dentistry was a very frustrating process to begin with. If patients were required to submit their own claims and made to spend hours ensuring the paperwork was correct, only to be told that it was wrongly coded or there was missing information, they would have gone on strike. Moreover, it would have given them a whole new outlook about billing errors and the sheer weight of the burdensome, backbreaking bureaucratic administration involved.

Every year a new codebook came out, with updates of new procedures and new descriptions of what those procedures were. Techniques changed with advances in materials, so coding itself continued to change with these technical changes. Some insurance companies paid for some codes and not others; each individual insurance company had a different repertoire of procedures it was uniquely willing to fund.

In dental school in the late 1980s, composites, or white-colored filling materials, were all the rage and were becoming very popular due to their many benefits for the patient. Many studies warned of the effects of mercury poisoning related to amalgam fillings, so the use of composites was already becoming the treatment of choice for most patients. Indeed, amalgam fillings were a necessary material to use at the time, but with more recent concerns about mercury poisoning, composites were an obvious improvement.

From a coding standpoint, if a dentist filled the tooth with composite, a composite code was used. Insurance companies, however, failed to recognize the use of composites for posterior teeth, those farthest back in the mouth. As students, we were told insurance companies didn't want the dental community to remove amalgam restorations and replace them with composite (despite the mercury risk). Amalgams still tended to last a little bit longer than composites, so the insurance company didn't want to pay to replace a perfectly good filling, which was understandable.

But this wasn't happening in practice. Maybe the insurance companies were worried they might face huge payouts if dentists embarked on a nationwide wholesale replacement of amalgams with composites, regardless of necessity.

No patient wanted unnecessary dental treatment, but even leaving aesthetics out of the argument, replacing amalgams with mercury-free composites was justifiable for pure health reasons. If the patients themselves really wanted their amalgams replaced with composites for health reasons, then why shouldn't they be allowed to do so? And if the dentist felt there was enough breakdown of the amalgam to warrant the replacement, then that would become a clinical necessity.

With the front teeth, using tooth-colored filling materials was a no-brainer, and insurance companies were more than happy to pay for them. But when it came to the posterior teeth, insurance companies were very reluctant to do the same for the higher-priced composites when an amalgam was cheaper. Hence, when a composite was submitted to the insurance company for payment, the insurance company would routinely change the code from a composite code to an amalgam code for payment.

This didn't mean the dentist was a fraud for coding a composite because that was what they'd provided. Equally, from an administrative perspective, it would have been logical for a dentist to code for an amalgam instead of a composite, to avoid the paperwork being delayed. In either case, there was absolutely no fraud involved.

A poll of dentists across the United States at the time would have revealed that a large percentage were billing a composite out as an amalgam, not because they were being fraudulent but because they knew they would only get paid for the amalgam (composites are generally about 25 percent more expensive than amalgams because they take longer to place, and materials cost more).

If a dentist wanted to give the patient a better service for less, in the full knowledge the insurance company was only required to pay the lower amount, where was the crime? Furthermore, if insurance companies changed the codes themselves to fit their payment procedures, how could dentists be held criminally liable for using the incorrect codes? Insane.

Another important point concerning Counts 1 through 9 was that the federal prosecutor had to show those treatment counts were somehow related to the union charge. But those patient files had absolutely nothing to do with the union. They were not members, nor did the FBI raid my files. I believe those files were obtained because Wendy needed to show them something so they would take the focus off her and place it on me.

My office manager called me on the day Wendy left my office for the last time, informing me Wendy had taken with her a garbage bag full of something that looked like papers. I immediately tried to contact Wendy to find out what she'd taken from the office, but she never answered my phone calls. So that was it. I never talked to her again.

I don't know for sure, but I think she had photocopied charts to provide to the FBI I had been engaged in some kind of fraudulent scheme. I imagine they must have pressured her to give them information on me to save her own skin. Removing unprotected patient files from an office is a crime. HIPAA, the Health Insurance Portability and Accountability Act of 1996, would be all over Wendy for doing so. The FBI may feel they're above the law, but they too would be in violation for accepting those records.

There had obviously been some kind of plan between my former associate, Wendy Fazzolari, and finally Julie. My gut feeling is Wendy planned the entire charade by telling the other two the FBI would soon be breathing down my neck, and the office would ultimately be closed down. She was, without a doubt in my mind, the instigator, running a renegade operation long before I became the target.

Before she left, I believe she had already been dealing with the FBI since 2005, when her sister-in-law blew her in, doing whatever she could to frame me to save her own skin and that of her husband. I'm certainly disappointed in my former associate, but Julie didn't have a mean bone in her body, so I don't believe she left my office so unexpectedly of her own accord. I'm certain it was because of Wendy's influence.

It wasn't until later I learned that Wendy was given immunity by the FBI to testify against me. They knew she'd done something wrong, like submitting a false bill to the union, and then worse, verifying that her husband's work was completed. There was no other reason to give her that immunity. My former associate may not have been so complicit, but she too was granted immunity from the feds for her aid in my case.

Both of them told the FBI I had been taking cash out of the practice every week. I did. I pulled aside $500 each week to pay my ex-wife my child support after the divorce. Yes, a check would have left a much better paper trail for the IRS to look at, but my accountant confirmed these monies were accounted for.

The FBI investigators went to meet with that accountant once and never went back, and for good reason. There was no tax fraud, but they still accused me of accepting undisclosed payments. That, and the overestimation of how much money I had overclaimed from Delta and other insurance companies, was how the FBI was able to add the counts of false accounting and tax fraud. It was also why they'd been so fixated on my credit adjustments during our initial meeting.

In reality, there was no tax offense of any kind. Each year I paid whatever tax my CPA instructed me to pay, no questions asked. My CPA was extremely conservative, so, if anything, I probably paid more than I should have, which was usually more than $120,000 annually.

The Department of Justice Criminal Tax Manual states the government must prove these things beyond reasonable doubt:

"First: That the Defendant owed substantial income tax in addition to the amount declared on [his] [her] tax return . . ."

"Second: That the Defendant knew when [he] [she] filed that income tax return that [he] [she] owed substantially more taxes than the amount reported on [his] [her] return."

And "Third: That the Defendant intended to evade paying taxes he knew he was required by law to pay."

Crucially, "The Government does not have to prove the precise amount of the additional tax due. But it must prove beyond a reasonable doubt that the Defendant knowingly and willfully attempted to evade or defeat paying a substantial part of the additional tax."

This gives the government a lot of leverage, since "substantial" is a relative term and need not be measured in terms of gross and net income or by any particular percentage of the tax shown to be due and payable. Also, as the courts have stated, the real character of the offense lies, not in the failure to file a return or in the filing of a false return, but rather in the intent to evade ANY tax.

The prosecution would have a difficult task in a court trial to prove beyond reasonable doubt that I deliberately evaded paying tax, but that didn't matter. All they were interested in was creating a long list of criminal charges to make me look guilty and scare me into taking a plea or otherwise risk a massive prison sentence.

During the discovery process, I uncovered another detail concerning my FBI interview that was a cause for concern. When they had asked me, "Well, Dr. Geise, is it possible Wendy could have made the bill for Tony?"

I had replied, "I have no idea. Ask them. Ask the Fazzolaris. I don't know who submitted the bill."

They had written in their notes that I had become nervous at that moment. They subsequently claimed the more they pushed me to say that Wendy had made the bill, the more nervous I became.

I have absolutely no recollection of being nervous, but I certainly remember being irritated that they repeatedly ignored me when I kept telling them the bill did not resemble a bill and should not have been accepted as such. It was not a bill. But being nervous about being guilty? That was ridiculous.

There was no intent on my part to do anything incorrect or dishonest, and certainly, I had no recollection of having done anything wrong, so how could my emotions have possibly been interpreted by three supposedly highly trained and intuitive FBI agents as "nervous"? And somehow that incriminated me?

Furthermore, in 2005, before I got wind of any FBI investigation or any trouble I might be in, I hired professional consulting help through Kristie with the express intention of making sure everything in my practice was being done correctly, down to the smallest detail and coding. So, by the end of 2005, I was coding composite fillings in a slightly different way, eliminating what I would call a grey area.

But those previous billings were something the FBI interpreted as serious criminality, specifically the crime of "misrepresentation." Hence, Counts 2 to 58 all fell between 2002 and 2005. Either way, wasn't my being proactive in hiring an independent dental accounting firm proof there was no intent to commit a crime? That alone should have been enough to undermine the charges unless they were simply trying to pile on enough risk to eventually get me to plea out.

I had my 30-year dental school reunion coming up in the fall, so I was trying to keep my legal battles out of my mind, at least for a little while. And that was when something good, actually great, was about to happen.

CHAPTER EIGHTEEN

MEETING MY FUTURE WIFE AND HER FAMILY

"Mr. Gorbachev, tear down this wall!"
-   President Ronald Reagan, Berlin Wall Speech

I heard Reagan's speech a year before I started serving my country in Germany, and when I arrived there, our main focus at that time was to ensure the Soviets didn't try to overrun us through the Fulda Gap. Thankfully, that never happened, and there was talk then that economic issues were wearing very heavily on our enemies.

The Soviet Union was already beginning to fall apart when the Berlin Wall came down, and many of the satellite countries had more than enough Russian influence. My soon-to-be wife, Larina, and her family (the Shtarkers) were from a small country in Eastern Europe called Moldova, the direct southern neighbor to Ukraine. Not unlike Newfane, it was a country that was known for its agriculture, growing mostly corn and harvesting grapes for wine, and during World War II it was gathered into the amalgamation of countries known as the USSR.

The Berlin Wall was built the same year I was born, in 1961, and I'm so fortunate to have been able to witness its fall first-hand. I also like to think my efforts on the West side of the Berlin Wall may have had some effect on the eventual dissolution of the Soviet Union.

Moldova was a very quiet and simple country, but, to be included in the mainstream of the Soviet economy, the Russians forced all their satellite countries to adopt the Cyrillic alphabet and speak Russian, no matter what age they were. The street signs all changed from Latin characters to Cyrillic, and the people of Moldova had to adopt a new first language, speaking only their mother tongue (Moldovan) in the safe confines of their own homes. How confusing that must have been. Just imagine if that were to happen here in the United States.

When I was traveling in Europe during my Army days, I managed to make it across the Iron Curtain to countries like Hungary, Romania, and Bulgaria, but never as far as the USSR, of which Moldova was a part at the time.

The Shtarkers had suffered through years of Soviet rule by staying very close to one another. They had a very strong family network that relied on helping each other in any way they could. When that wall finally did come down, they were able to see an opening my future in-laws decided to take and so began the process of seeking asylum in the United States.

In 1989, the Shtarkers began applying for refugee status with the US Embassy. They too had heard of all the stories of immigrants fleeing their own countries in search of a better life in America, and they were prepared to do whatever was needed and to wait as long as it took to find out for themselves. They were also well aware of the corrupt government of the Soviet Union and were hopeful America really stood behind what they said, "One nation under God, indivisible, with liberty and justice for all."

"Give me your tired, your poor, your huddled masses

yearning to breathe free, the wretched refuse of your teeming shore, send these the homeless, tempest-tossed to me. . ." These words, sacrosanct to all immigrants, were engraved on the Statue of Liberty, the first proclamation of freedom as immigrants reached the NY Harbor on their way to Ellis Island.

But before the Shtarkers could make that journey, they would have to take care of countless things in their native country, including filing paperwork with the United States. That meant traveling to Moscow to fill out their paperwork in person and being interviewed at the US embassy there. Moscow had the only embassy for all the former Soviet countries, so they all had to pass through Russia to get out. It cost each of them a month's salary just to apply to leave, but they were more than ready to spend everything they had to seek a better life.

From that interview, the Shtarkers waited two full years before hearing any kind of response from the United States, but once they were given word they had received refugee status, they now had to sell everything they couldn't carry in their personal luggage, which had to be a certain size and shape for travel. Alex and Frida, my parents-in-law, had a tailor make each of them a bag of the exact dimensions they had been given so there would be no question when they reached Moscow. But they would also be traveling with their children, Larina and Yan, and Frida's parents. They needed assistance for Frida's father because of a recent stroke, so the six of them arranged for a flight that had some medical coverage aboard.

At home in Moldova, they started the process of selling their home and anything else they wouldn't be taking with them. They had to work out arrangements with their local government to show they had sold or given away everything they owned, except for the luggage they could carry. They would only be allowed to step on the plane with $100 per person, and Frida's parents were counted separately because they had a different last name. I can't imagine having to leave everything behind and starting over with virtually nothing, but they knew it would be the best decision of their lives, so they pressed on.

As they took the 23-hour train ride again to Moscow and awaited the opportunity to board their flight, the customs officers there decided the luggage was too big, so they charged Alex $100 for the extra baggage. Talk about criminal! But what could they do at that point other than smile and pay? So, the Shtarkers found themselves entering the U.S. with only $300, but, fortunately, some of Alex's family was already here. As a tribute to my future family, I appreciate how they never took a single cent from our government programs.

Not one of them believed the United States owed them anything, so they went to work anywhere they could. At that time, the minimum wage was $4.25 an hour, and their apartment cost $375 a month for rent. Each week, they pooled their money, put $35 toward food, and the rest went toward their debt to the United States. They were determined to pay it all off within one year. They went to school, took out student loans, cleaned hotel rooms, drove taxis, and spent very little on unnecessary things. They never ate out or went to the movies because they had to pay the United States back for their flights to get here.

It was 1995, and, in just three years, due to their

enormous strength, fortitude, frugality, and diligence, they were able to buy a house of their own here in America. I'm so proud of their story, especially knowing they have seen both sides of the Iron Curtain and have worked harder than the vast majority of people I know, all in search of a better life here in America.

In October 2008, I was fixed up on a blind date with that same beautiful young woman by the name of Larina Shtarker, just a few days before my 30-year Dental School Reunion.

CHAPTER NINETEEN

SNOOPING AROUND THE UNION

"There is nothing more deceptive than an obvious fact."
-    Arthur Conan Doyle

I found it staggering that here we were so far down the road to a criminal trial, and yet not once had anyone tried to find out which individual or group of individuals actually paid the alleged "bill" that Tony allegedly submitted.

By now I was convinced there had to be someone crooked (rather than merely incompetent) working on the inside to sign off on patently fake bills. There was no way the "bill" that Tony had given me in the fall of 2005 could have been signed off any other way. As stated before, it had no dates of service, no coding to explain what was done, no charges other than numbers without dollar signs, and no signature confirming the work had been completed.

The FBI and US attorneys prosecuting the case certainly were aware of this, so I ran this reality past my attorney, Mr. Daniels. Initially, he deflected my request by listing all the people he knew over at the union and stressing he couldn't imagine any of them could be complicit in a crime (even though just a few years earlier the FBI had convicted 18 union members, including

Tony's business partner, Mr. M).

Why Mr. Daniels was more intent on vouching for their less than impeccable reputations, rather than doing his job and defending mine, remained—and still remains—a mystery to me. I didn't believe Daniels was covering anything up; he just seemed, well, half-assed about its significance. If it had been the other way around, and I had been my own attorney, I'd have been down at the union like a dog at a bone, causing a scene and refusing to leave until somebody gave me the information I needed.

That's one of the major frustrations of being a defendant in a criminal case fighting for your freedom and facing a lifetime behind bars. Everyone keeps telling you to sit on your hands, to do nothing, to be patient, and to let your defense attorney do what they do best: defend you. Meanwhile, the government juggernaut just kept rolling forward, slowly crushing me—an innocent man—under its wheels.

"Look," I said to Mr. Daniels, pressing him again, "*somebody* at the union paid Tony. If we can get the proof that whoever paid him didn't follow the correct procedure or didn't scrutinize the bill properly, then clearly it's an internal matter at the union and not because I committed a brilliant forgery that fooled everybody so Tony could get his money, which did not benefit me one iota. So you need to get down there and find out how they were paid and who paid them. I mean, wouldn't that be the first thing the FBI should have looked at?"

Mr. Daniels finally relented. He said he would check things out at the union and get back to me. Within a week, he responded with his tail between his legs. "Well, er . . .

you know what?" he said. "There's just not a whole lot to go on there." So that was the end of that, maybe the most important inquiry in my case as regards Count 1.

Then, out of the blue, in early March 2009, an anonymous handwritten letter arrived at my office. The writer expressed sympathy for my predicament, wished me luck, and lamented that I had been put in such a terrible position and that they would do anything to help if they could. The letter advised me to approach the union to pull up their records to show how they had drawn down from their welfare fund to date (something my attorney still had not been able to accomplish).

I subsequently learned the letter had been sent by none other than Tony Fazzolari's father. I only found this out because I ran into a guy in Newfane, who was married to Tony's sister, Gina. John had said, "Doc, we really feel for you. Listen, my father-in-law said he sent you a letter. He's on his deathbed, and he's really concerned about setting things straight."

Mr. Fazzolari could obviously see his son and suspect daughter-in-law hadn't taken responsibility for their actions and were pinning the blame on me. Why else would he get involved?

I replied, "So sorry to hear about your father-in-law, John, and I'm glad he knows what's happening, but what can I do with this?"

"All you have to do is go to the union" John replied. "They'll show you what Tony and Wendy have taken out of their welfare fund."

So that's what I did. Without notifying my attorneys, I hired a private detective to go to the union to find out that exact information. A few days later, as soon as my attorneys got wind of this, that someone was snooping around the union on my behalf, they finally decided to get off their asses and do it themselves. They came back with some very revealing information.

First of all, the union accounts weren't insurance policies, like the FBI had led everyone to believe. They were more like savings accounts or rainy-day funds. Union members could pay money in, tax-free, and then take it out again when they needed it—anything from home improvements to vacations. But, crucially, they had to pay tax on any withdrawals, unless the money was used to pay medical bills. Moreover, to keep the account open, members had to keep a minimum of $1,000 in their accounts.

My attorneys eventually discovered the Fazzolaris had made several withdrawals throughout the years, each accompanied by a medical bill. Each time they made a withdrawal, the balance remaining would always be $1,000 to the penny. So clearly these medical bills were tailored to extract the maximum amount of money rather than accurately reflecting any work done. Tony's bill for $6,970 fit this same pattern: once it had been paid, exactly $1,000 remained in the account. They didn't steal money—it was their own money all along—but they had created false bills to avoid paying taxes.

The amazing thing is they had been making these same withdrawals for many years, long before I ever met them or entered the picture. They had forged and used other doctors' stationery in the same manner. In my case, they submitted an old piece of stationery from my previous office address (where I was formerly located in January 2002). That particular stationery had all been thrown out the year before when I made the move to the new office address in May 2001.

In addition to that, the prosecutor had charged me with the crime of aiding and abetting the embezzling of money from the Local 91 Union Welfare Fund. That law was in place to prevent the union leadership from dipping into their members' accounts, not for members taking money out of their own. Once again, these FBI agents had orchestrated the appearance of a much bigger story by fabricating a crime that I didn't commit, and could not commit, unless I was a union leader.

Sidney Powell's words about prosecutor malfeasance were beginning to hit home with me—that Fabrication Beats Investigation. The government employees in question had allowed their desire for praise from their superiors to take precedence over their moral duty not to prosecute an innocent man—and seek to put him in jail for over 100 years. Or, as the Doobie Brother's song goes, "What a fool believes, he sees!"

The Fazzolaris were simply trying to beat the system by not paying tax on their withdrawals, which the IRS might be concerned about, but as far as my involvement was concerned, there was no crime. So how could I aid and abet a nonexistent crime, especially if I wasn't there during the withdrawal?

I was ecstatic. I couldn't believe that, after all this time, and years of gut-wrenching worry, my attorneys had finally been able to uncover the vital evidence that I had been banging my head on for so many months. I knew the answers had always been in the union records. So, as part of the required disclosures right before the trial, in June 2009, we presented this important discovery information to the government, which quickly prompted their request for a court hearing.

I assumed the day I had been waiting for had finally arrived—the day when the government finally saw the bigger picture and dropped the case. But boy oh boy was I wrong. How could I have been so naive? During that court hearing, the government backpedaled and simply asked the judge to table Count 1 (the count for which we had spent the last six months preparing to defend), and instead substitute Counts 2 to 58.

At that point, the judge forcefully stated to the prosecution, "I'm sorry, but didn't you choose to go after Count 1 this past January?"

"Yes, Your Honor," the prosecution said, "but we now feel we should proceed with Counts 2 through 58 instead." Simple as that.

In truth, the government had the proof in front of them that I had been set up as the fall guy, and they now knew that charge was going nowhere. We had produced evidence that blew their case out of the water, so now they also wanted to seal all documents associated with Count 1 and shift the goalposts mid-game.

Was that even legal? I wondered. Or was it an attempt to cover up the fact they had fabricated a crime from whole cloth when I had absolutely nothing to do with the administration of Local 91?

In addition, all of a sudden, the government submitted a motion to disqualify my attorney, Mr. Daniels, for an alleged conflict of interest. I couldn't help but wonder whether this was the reason he originally couldn't find anything at Local 91 that could benefit my defense.

The motion called for a so-called *Curcio* hearing, used

to determine if one of the government's star witnesses had created a conflict of interest for the defense attorney. As part of the motion, the government argued I should be assigned a public defender so they could still use their star witness. So, on July 6, I had to return to the courthouse to meet a new attorney who would explain my rights to conflict-free counsel.

I had to decide whether I should abandon Mr. Daniels and get a new attorney or sign the waiver of my rights. As far as I was concerned, we had the government beaten, and now they were doing anything they could to disrupt what I thought would be a slam-dunk for dismissal. So, I decided to keep my team in place and signed the waiver.

As a result, the trial of Count 1 was postponed. Then, on July 8, the court made an entry in the official docket: "Sealed document as to Scott D. Geise."

But now, shouldn't the severed Counts 2 through 58 be presented to the grand jury, isolated and alone from all of the other counts, to see if there's enough evidence to warrant a new indictment for those charges? In my interpretation of the law, the Federal Rules of Criminal Justice, and the Constitution of the United States, it sure says they do.

Since the judge had granted severance back in January 2009, if Counts 2 through 58 were now going to be pursued, the government was required to put them before a grand jury to see if there was any merit to the prosecutor's case on just those counts alone. But they didn't because there was no complaint to begin with. The same applied to Counts 59 to 65—a separate grand jury matter entirely—but, despite this, no one was there to ensure the law was followed.

I knew this couldn't be right, so I instructed my attorney to immediately submit a motion for dismissal. The judge ultimately rejected it, cancelling the July 3, 2009, trial date and continuing the trial to March 3, 2010. I was in shock, totally beyond myself, and if I'm entirely honest, at this time I viewed America's federal legal system with absolute disgust.

By now, moreover, the financial cost of defending myself had been devastating. And harder to quantify, the emotional and psychological cost had also been horrific. I was angry and frustrated that we'd come so close to getting the case dismissed, and now I had to spend another nine months preparing for a completely different trial.

Fairness? I don't think so. And it bears saying again: whatever happened to a speedy trial, one of the fundamental rights in the American jurisprudence system? When the government has unlimited resources, why should the accused have to wait until the government can find or fabricate something to convict him? That's why Congress enacted the Speedy Trial Act in the first place, and that's why a speedy trial is mandated by the Bill of Rights in the Fifth, Sixth, Seventh, and Eighth Amendments to the Constitution.

Meanwhile, to make things worse, the lawsuit over my damaged boat (I certainly could have used the money) was going nowhere. The insurance company refused to pay me for the damage the Coast Guard had inflicted on my boat, and they even argued I had damaged the boat myself to claim the entire value as a write-off. In other words, they accused me of insurance fraud. This pattern was becoming depressingly familiar. In the end, we lost the boat, and, with it a piece of history, and I remained responsible for the remaining $360,000 on the boat loan.

It was around this time I made a chilling discovery that confirmed my growing suspicion that the reckless destruction of my boat and the subsequent accusation of insurance fraud—had been more than monumental bad luck. I learned MM—one of the three FBI agents who had first interviewed me in February 2006, and who then had bullied and verbally abused my cleaner Sherry because she wouldn't let them into my office—also held another important law enforcement position in the local community. He was none other than an intelligence operative for the US Coast Guard.

In the beginning, MM had been one of my dental patients. Although I had never actually treated him for any major dental work, he had maintained his six-month hygiene program with Wendy Fazzolari. She was the only person in my practice with whom he ever had contact. In fact, he refused to see any of the other hygienists in the practice, insisting on Wendy.

It was around this time that I also discovered Wendy spent more than ample time with MM, at every appointment, and would often run late with her next patients, presumably because she was focused on MM so heavily. I hadn't put two and two together until this point. I have since learned the other women in the office often made fun of how Wendy would spend so much more time with MM when he was in her chair than with other patients.

Maybe this was where they cooked up a deal to take me down in exchange for making the Fazzolaris' charges disappear. MM knew Wendy and Tony received the funds directly, and that Newfane Family Dentistry had not submitted anything for them, nor verified that treatment had been completed for anything that was on my stationery.

I struggle to see why I, of all people, became his target. Did he have a beef with me that I wasn't aware of? Wendy certainly had a motive, which was to save her own skin, but I still don't understand why MM decided to pursue me when it should have been so obvious there was zero evidence of any wrongdoing on my behalf.

MM had also been highly commended for his involvement in the FBI's take down of the leadership of the Local 91 for racketeering and extortion. As a result, he had become very powerful, very untouchable, and very unimpeachable in his efforts and determination to bury me.

MM was a prime example of toxic masculinity, and he certainly thought of himself as some kind of an Italian stallion. Former partners told stories of his alleged aggression toward women and of his passion for being "in the game." I suspect no one in our close-knit community would have put it past him to have leveraged Wendy for certain favors in return for taking the heat off her own union fraud.

Whether this happened or not, I don't know for a fact. Wendy would have had to give him something in return, something that would allow him to pursue a bigger fish if possible, within the union, or possibly the avenue that could bring me down during the time Medicare and Medicaid fraud were a law enforcement priority.

It was either going to be her ass, or mine, I suspect, and I believe MM worked the system so he could have both.

~

The government prepared for the new trial date by visiting every patient listed in Counts 2 to 58. They took photographs of the teeth of each patient to prove, in each case, that I had failed to provide an amalgam filling. Never mind that, in each case, the patient would say, "I can confirm Dr. Geise gave me the filling."

Ironically, these restorations didn't show up on the photographs because they were white composite fillings that were color matched to the individual tooth and barely showed up. This was unlike a grey amalgam filling. That's why modern dentists have been using white composite fillings instead of ugly grey amalgam fillings for decades now.

At first, the government was happily snapping the insides of the mouths of all these potential witnesses and were delighted to find what looked to be no fillings, proving I hadn't done the work. But, as they interviewed more and more of my patients, I think eventually the sledgehammer must have dropped, and they must have realized their mistake. I had indeed performed every single one of those 57 fillings, albeit with a white composite instead of the amalgam.

So, the prosecutors changed their approach. Now they argued it was still fraud because the work I had done didn't match what I had claimed. This was a highly technical position, depending on dental nuances, but they still believed they had their fraud case. Indeed, they planned to call every single one of those patients in as a witness, to testify I had supplied them with something different to that which I had claimed from the insurance company.

By the way, none of my patients had any complaints about the work, but, to the government, that didn't matter. All that mattered was the optics of the government prosecutors being able to tee up dozens of witnesses to support their fraud case. And, it looked bad for me, my attorney said, that the government was able to call all these people to testify to my guilt.

But, at the same time, some patients felt comfortable enough to call and inform me of what was happening: That the FBI investigators were trying to put words into their mouths to try to hang me. One patient called me in tears to tell me the FBI wanted her to say I had pushed her into getting treatment when she didn't need or want it. Which was completely absurd!

The government couldn't even argue the insurance company should not have paid me for my claims. The insurance company paid me for the amalgam in each case in the full knowledge I did a composite, which cost more. So I was fully entitled to receive that money. But all the government had to do to show an intent on my part to defraud was to go through all my files and hunt for a single instance where I billed and received more money than I should have.

And what do you know? After sifting through all the bills—and all of the 89,000+ procedures I had completed during that time—the government managed to find only one single occasion where my office had accidentally charged the insurance company for an amalgam filling when a hygienist had actually supplied a cheaper sealant (about $20 cheaper). The work had been billed incorrectly, which was merely an administrative error.

It is inevitable that, when you're issuing thousands of bills each year, a few errors will occur. The government found it, and this is all they needed to prove I was a criminal because they had the almighty credibility and force of the federal government on their side. The supreme irony was the person who made that administrative error, by billing for an amalgam instead of a sealant, was none other than Wendy Fazzolari.

CHAPTER TWENTY

FEDERAL JURY TRIAL: DAY ONE

"A jury consists of twelve persons chosen to decide who has the better lawyer."

- Robert Frost

Buffalo's federal court building is a grand old structure built in 1936. It has a very unusual shape due to the real estate it was built upon. The architects created a pentagonal-shaped, seven-story building, very different from the traditional rectangular blocks seen throughout the city. The cornerstone was laid by Federal Judge John K. Hazel on May 29, 1936, and it was dedicated in person by our nation's acting president, Franklin D. Roosevelt, on October 17, 1936.

President Roosevelt took office on March 4, 1933, almost 77 years before day one of my trial in this esteemed federal courthouse. The proceedings would be a test of the very system President Roosevelt presided over for almost 14 years. FDR, as he was commonly called, was a man built on solid principles, and one who never forgot that constitutional rights actually meant something.

Whatever documents were sealed in July must have been to the benefit of the government because, for the better part of the nine months leading up to trial, the government continued to beg the courts to allow them to add Count 1 back into their case, filing motion after motion, even after the severance had been firmly granted. However, by February 8, 2010, the court was tired of listening to the government's arguments and thus denied their motion once and for all.

At 8:15 a.m., when I approached the courthouse steps on my first day of trial, one of the security guards had just stepped outside to prop open the exterior glass door. This old building had troubles of its own, and the air conditioning was broken again. The courthouse was also in need of some pretty urgent repairs, and a gentle breeze from street level wafting into my face was a refreshing contrast to the discomfort I anticipated the day would bring.

The security guard set a weighted pedestal in place, turned around just at the right moment, and continued to hold open the door as I entered. I walked inside and patted my dress shirt pocket to check nothing metal was hiding within. The monumental first-floor lobby was now in full view, with the security desk and metal detectors poised and ready for a busy day.

The press had arrived early and were set up across from the elevators as I dropped my keys, phone, watch, and wallet into the bin on the conveyor belt and proceeded through the framed metal detector. I placed my briefcase on the conveyor belt, checked my pockets one last time, and then walked through, mindful I was crossing a significant threshold. Events unfolding in this building over the next few days would determine my precious freedom.

"Please silence your phone, sir," said one of the guards as he handed back the bin full of my belongings. I checked my phone and gave him a smile and a nod.

"Thank you," the guard said, "have a great day."

As I rechecked the time on my watch and walked across the polished marble floor toward the elevator doors, I could sense the invasive curiosity of both a reporter and a cameraman. I imagined them as jackals, sniffing the air for fresh meat. I looked down at the paperwork in my right hand to double-check that nothing was legible and stared intently at the elevator light. Moments later, the doors slid open, and I stepped inside, pushing the button for the second floor as the elevator doors closed.

I savored this brief moment of solitude, feeling the sound of my heart beating firmly in my chest. Today was the first day of trial, so the agenda was busy, choosing and swearing in the jury from a pool of 100 people. Three years of delays and U-turns and starts and stops had finally culminated in my day—or, more accurately, my month—in court.

Mr. Muscato was waiting for me in the empty courtroom. I was ridiculously early, with proceedings scheduled to start at 9:00 a.m. He greeted me with a wide smile and an overconfident handshake and said, "Well, Doc, you made it to the big time. We're in Federal Court now. That's the biggest of the big." I couldn't work out whether he was trying to put me at ease or scare the crap out of me to get me to plea at the last minute.

A few steps inside the courtroom conjured visions of opulence harking back to one of the most difficult times in American history, the Depression. The vast stretches of ornate woodwork could be seen along the marble floors, and up the walls, framing an impressive ceiling, adorned with chandeliers and decorative plaster work. It was a job well done because it certainly gave the impression of government supremacy and power.

The whole place was very intimidating. I'm sure our voices would have echoed if we'd been talking any louder, but everything in that courtroom was designed to challenge the ego of the ordinary man and woman, ensuring total compliance.

I found myself talking in hushed tones, almost a whisper, and my heart was already beating faster than usual in anticipation of the hours ahead. As I sat in that huge empty chamber at the defense table, although I felt awestruck, I also felt momentarily bolstered, as if the solidity and cold impartiality of the architecture formed a sentinel of justice that would protect me from injustice.

We weren't alone for long, and, by 8:50 a.m., a parade of people were entering the court. The government's cadre of attorneys were all dressed in grey suits and carried briefcases, like a small juridical army. Emerging from different directions, court staff started to fill the room. Two middle-aged women walked through a door on the side of the courtroom, one being the judge's administrative assistant, and the other being the court reporter. They took their seats just below the lofty judge's bench.

No sooner was the room buzzing with a dozen hushed conversations than we were called to order. As we rose in silence, Judge Richard Arcara glided into the courtroom from chambers, looking like he'd just come from doing something important, his black robe billowing slightly as he laid claim to the large mahogany throne facing us at the front of the court.

Federal judges are nominated by the President of the United States and confirmed by the Senate. Barring no bad behavior, they're appointed for life and bestowed an annual salary of $174,000, plus benefits. A judge who has reached the age of 65 (or has become disabled) may retire or elect to go on Senior Status and keep working if they so desire. This freedom allows all District Court judges to be as unbiased as humanly possible, able to withstand pressures from all sides and do what is right and just.

Judge Arcara must have been in his early 70s. His round face, with its bald forehead, thin lips, and wide nose could have sat equally at home on the shoulders of a trade union leader or a chief of police, but his complexion was disarmingly soft. He reminded me of Tony Soprano, only older. With a half-frown, he rapidly swept the chamber with his languid but commanding gaze, nodded to the staff who were sitting one level below him, and then issued his first command: "Please be seated."

Clearing her throat, the court clerk then asked if we were ready for the trial. As soon as we said we were ready, the levees broke, and the courtroom doors opened to the 100 potential jurors, who filed in and took virtually every seat available—people from all walks of life, of all different races and colors, the proverbial ordinary jury of your peers.

So began the long process called *voir dire* (meaning in French, " to speak the truth"), during which Judge Arcara questioned each potential juror, one by one, to determine their suitability to serve on the jury. The purpose of this was to exclude from the jury people who were unable or unsuitable for whatever reason to decide the case fairly. Usually, it was a matter of eliminating those who might know someone involved in the case—or if they had prior information that would influence or prejudice their judgment and, more generally, for the attorneys to reject anyone with strong bias either way.

When all the potential jurors were seated, Judge Arcara addressed them collectively. He informed them of their solemn duty to uphold justice, and he gave a brief outline of the case, including the small detail that the prosecution would be calling 80 different witnesses to support its 65-count indictment, which asserted I had illegally accepted over $120,000 in fraudulent payments from the insurance carriers.

The judge asked if there was anyone present who felt he was unable to be unbiased in the event he was one of the 12 selected for the trial or one of the alternates. Potential juror #3 was the first of maybe a dozen people to raise their hands.

The judge asked him to stand up. "Your Honor," he said. "You have just turned around and told us the government has 65 counts against the defendant and is going to call 80 prosecution witnesses. Even with countervailing evidence, how could I not think the man was guilty? How can 80 people be wrong?"

The man sat down again, clearly feeling quite pleased with himself for having used the phrase "countervailing evidence." He glanced proudly at some of the other potential jurors as if inviting their admiration at his boldness and perspicacity. He was clearly an avid watcher of *Law & Order* and probably fancied himself a shoo-in for juror foreman.

The judge immediately dismissed him from jury service, but that man had just voiced my deepest fear about this whole circus. I wondered how many more of the potential jury members felt the same way and wouldn't be honest or brave enough to admit it. I knew the optics looked bad for me. With 65 counts and 80 witnesses against me, I looked guilty as hell, and the government knew it—because it was all part of their strategy.

After dismissing two pregnant women, the judge embarked on the lengthy process of interviewing every single juror (a process that would last the rest of the day). Some conversations were very brief, whereas others fell into the realm of absurdity. One young woman, Potential Juror #33, said she had three young children at home, and, when asked about what they were doing, she replied she had left them watching *SpongeBob SquarePants* with her mother.

The judge peered quizzically over his reading glasses. "SpongeBob who?"

"SpongeBob SquarePants, Your Honor."

A ripple of muted laughter spread around the room.

"Square pants, pants like the pants you wear?"

"Yes, Your Honor. It's a very popular cartoon these days."

The judge exchanged an embarrassed glance with his court assistant.

"SpongeBob SquarePants?" He shook his head and smiled as he repeated the name. "Does anyone else know anything about this show?"

Potential Juror #20 raised his hand. He was quick to state he had five children under the age of nine, and he was very familiar with the show. He explained SpongeBob was an actual sea sponge that lived at the bottom of the ocean, and that Bikini Bottom was his home. "The reason he is called SpongeBob SquarePants, Your Honor, is because he is a square yellow sponge, and the only pants he could possibly wear were also square."

Despite these bizarre moments of levity, another potential jury member—#67—stuck in my memory for a more sinister reason. The judge had told the courtroom the trial would last about a month, and when this one guy had his turn in front of the judge, he said he was a truck driver, and he couldn't afford to take a month off work, and that he needed to be excused from jury service so he could take an important trucker's driving test and thus provide for his family.

Judge Arcara spent a lot of time asking this particular guy questions. The judge explained that, for our system to work, we all have to make sacrifices from time to time, and he didn't feel this test was anything that couldn't be rescheduled, so a dismissal was out of the question. The trucker sat down, now even more aggravated.

The process continued for the rest of the day. Each side was allowed to choose to dismiss three potential jurors from the list of possible jurors without stating a reason. This is called a "peremptory challenge." The defense could dismiss those they felt would be damaging to their case, and the government had the power to do the same. The ones who remained were fair game to become the determinants of my fate.

By the end of the day, #67, the trucker, was still in the eligible pool, and my defense team selected him for the final jury. When he realized he'd been picked, the poor guy's face fell to the floor. He clenched his fists and glared over at my defense attorneys as if they'd ruined his life. I remember thinking that having a juror already feeling very aggrieved at my team could be yet another potential problem.

The government attorneys and my defense counsel had whittled the 100 down to just 12 jurors and an alternate, someone who could stand in for any juror who was unable to continue their service during the trial. It had been a very long day, and my mother had endured it all. She'd heard all the *voir dire* and all of the begging for recusal, and she understood her son's professional life was hanging in the balance. Tomorrow would include the opening statements, as well as the government's presentation of evidence.

As the judge explained again about the importance of the duty that each juror would be faced with throughout the trial, he attempted to alleviate some of their fears and apprehensions by again commenting on the integrity of the system of law within the United States—that one of our duties as Americans is to participate in the judicial system in cases like these, and that their role was crucial for justice to work.

Judge Arcara then excused the remaining jurors, who were led out of the box through a side door. They filed out one by one, and while most of the jurors felt a little embarrassed about the procession, they kept their eyes focused somewhat straight ahead.

As for Juror #67, however, Mr. Daniels commented, "Did you see the look he just gave me? I think he's going to be a problem."

CHAPTER TWENTY-ONE

FEDERAL JURY TRIAL: DAYS TWO AND THREE

"The course of justice often prevents it."
—Edward Counsel

The next morning, Wednesday, March 3, 2010, I stopped by my dental office to check the schedule and to see who would be coming in that day during my absence. It was still dark outside as I locked the office doors and stepped back into my car. Then I made the hour-long drive to Buffalo, parked my car, walked the quarter mile to the courthouse, and arrived in the courtroom 15 minutes early.

The second day began with the jury being sworn in and with opening statements, which is where both sides' attorneys lay out their case—and what they intend to prove. The courtroom was a bit quieter today, now with only the government prosecution team on one side, and my defense team, Mr. Daniels and Mr. Muscato, on the other.

Only two members of the public were in the viewing gallery: my parents, impeccably dressed, faces drained of color. We nodded sternly at each other.

The prosecution inevitably painted me as the next Al Capone. I include here some excerpts from the

DR SCOTT GEISE

prosecution's Trial Memorandum, which was filed before the trial and in which the government gave a brief "Summary of the Facts":

"The Indictment alleges the defendant engaged in a scheme to defraud insurance companies and dental benefit plans by submitting claim forms for payment for dental services he did not perform and for dental products the patients did not receive and need. Specifically, the Indictment charges that the defendant applied sealants to the teeth of certain patients—a procedure not covered by the patients' insurance plans—but which Geise then billed to the insurance companies as amalgams (silver fillings), which were covered by the patients' insurance plans. In addition, some of Geise's patients were given bleach whitening kits at no charge and which were not covered under the insurance plans, and then Geise's dental practice billed the patients' insurance companies for occlusal guards, which are prescribed to individuals who suffer from nocturnal bruxism (teeth grinding), and which were covered under the patients' insurance plans. Geise's dental practice billed $350 for each occlusal guard, and the typical insurance payment was approximately $255."

There are several details worth highlighting here: First, notice the emotive phrase, *"engaged in a scheme."* I can honestly say I had no intention to defraud, let alone to *"engage* in a *scheme."* If I had planned to defraud, I wouldn't have done it in plain sight, and I would have made sure I benefitted personally. Judging by what the government pulled out of all my patient files, it looked like there were a total of 30 occlusal guards over five years—or six incidents per year. Not much of a get-rich scheme.

I'd also like to draw attention to the phrase, *"dental services he did not perform."* From the get-go, that assertion planted a false idea into the minds of the jury. The reality was that, as I have explained earlier, I performed dental services that were far superior to those for which I billed the insurance company because old-fashioned amalgam fillings were inferior to modern white composites and therefore fell short of best practices.

I received the lesser figure from the insurance companies (with their full knowledge since they would routinely reject the claim for the composite, change the code, and pay me for an amalgam instead). My business made up the differential. There was no personal gain, and there was no hoodwinking of the insurance companies. No insurance companies complained or raised any issue of fraud; the only suggestion I had performed criminal acts came solely from the FBI and the government prosecutors. My motivation was always to offer my patients the best and most up-to-date service possible.

Second, I'd like to deconstruct the phrase *"dental products the patients did not receive and need."* Once again, there's an implication I duped insurance companies into paying for certain procedures while I sat and read a newspaper. Furthermore, at no time did I provide patients with services they *"did not . . . need."* I manufactured and billed for occlusal guards and offered my patients the added expense of *"bleach whitening kits at no charge."*

Once again, I did not personally benefit from this arrangement. So where was my motive to defraud? Despite the fact my so-called *scheme* intentionally left me financially worse off, the final sentence of the opening statement implied I was desperate for money, having just opened my new office: "*The defendant's fraudulent activity coincided with the opening of his new dentist office, which was much larger, and included more equipment, than his previous office.*"

How curious, then, that my *fraudulent activity* didn't make me any extra money to pay for this new equipment; instead, it intentionally left me financially worse off.

My attorney, Mr. Daniels, was next. He stood up and made his opening statement, but I found it worrisomely weak and hollow. He pointed out that I had never committed a crime in my life, that I ran a large successful dental practice in my hometown, and that I was an integral member of my community, having lived there all my life. He even mentioned I was coaching the school lacrosse team. He very much focused on my role in the community and how the trial was taking me away from serving it.

A key point to mention here in my defense is that, in 2001, my business started using a new computer programming software called Dentrix. The following description appeared in my pretrial submissions:

"This is a sophisticated dental computerized system. Each operatory has its own computer. The screen shows not only the patient's chart but also a picture of the patient's mouth as well as X-rays. Following treatment, the dental assistant inputs the appropriate treatment information into the computer, as reflected in the chart. A billing code is entered for the treatment. The software program will not produce a billing statement without a dental code billing reference. At the end of a day's office hours, all insurance billings are 'batched' and sent electronically to a clearing house which selects the appropriate carrier for billing."

Herein lies the problem: *"The software program will not produce a billing statement without a dental code billing reference."* So we had to provide a billing code, even if it didn't exactly fit the work we'd done; it was the closest we could get. Without a code, however imperfect, we couldn't bill anything, we couldn't send the statement off for clearing, and we couldn't log off and go home every evening. Like any system, it was imperfect, so you had to use your initiative and supply the software with the closest match to the treatment that had actually been performed.

After the opening statements, the prosecution called an expert witness. Dr. Timothy R. was a dentist who graduated from the same dental school I did. His testimony took an entire day, as he went through patient-by-patient and stated in each case how he would have coded differently from me. He also provided what the court termed "educational testimony to facilitate the jury's understanding of relevant dental terms, procedures, and practices, including the differences between bleach whitening kits and occlusal guards" (as if anyone was in any doubt that these were two separate things, but of course, it served the optics to get an expert witness to reiterate this, as if the obvious fact that they were patently different items was definitive proof of an intent to defraud on my part).

Dr. R also testified that, after having reviewed the X-rays of my patients, it was his opinion these patients did not have amalgams on their teeth. Of course, they didn't. I had never disputed that. Instead, they had received far superior, modern, and more expensive white composites at my cost (for the difference between the two).

Ironically, the more the "expert witness" talked, the more wrong he was, and I wrote down all his mistakes. By the middle of the second day, I had managed to fill an entire legal pad with my notes full of his factual inaccuracies. I couldn't wait to jump on all of this with my lawyers that evening so we could come back on Friday and set the record straight.

Then I looked over at my lawyers and a knot of anxiety began to grow in my stomach. Hour by hour, I realized I wasn't going to be allowed to even play this game of charades, let alone win. My attorneys sat stoically, their faces already etched with a mixture of disinterest and defeat. From their viewpoint, regardless of the weakness of the prosecution's argument, the optics were horrible, and I was starting to feel like the fall guy I'd always suspected myself to be.

No matter that Count 1—aiding and abetting union depositors to steal from their welfare fund—had been sealed and abandoned. No matter that Tony Fazzolari's ridiculous and falsified "bill" had begun this entire nightmare. That had been the government's main exhibit; the rest of the charges were icing on the cake. No matter then, that in the absence of an actual cake, this absurd prosecution was now relying entirely on the icing. And nobody seemed to care that the government had completely ignored the rules that were provided by Congress to provide a fair trial.

Morale was already tangibly poor in my camp when the prosecution lit the fuse under their one accurate count out of 65. They presented as evidence a single billing that showed my office had overcharged an insurance company for an amalgam filling when the handwritten dental records showed we had actually supplied a *cheaper* sealant. It had been billed incorrectly, entered by a hygienist on her own operatory computer. It was an administrative error, by none other than my ex-hygienist, Wendy Fazzolari, but it was damning, nonetheless.

My lawyers continued to reiterate that, if I were found guilty on this one count, then by force of implication I would most likely be found guilty on the other 57 counts (since Count #1 had been dropped and this trial was focused specifically on Counts 2 through 58). It was an accidental discrepancy of $23, but that was irrelevant. Legally, it might be proof of fraud, however small. Common sense would lead me to believe an error of this kind would be looked at just like it was—an error. But when this piece of evidence came before the court, my attorneys visibly slumped in defeat, slipping further into their chairs.

When we adjourned into our private study at the courthouse that evening, all my legal team would discuss was that sealant invoice. On the strength of that evidence alone, they thought we were going to lose, and that I should try for a plea bargain so I didn't face the possibility of 100+ years of prison time. They had also conveniently opened up materials from the Delta Dental insurance company that were in plain view when I walked in.

Specifically, the materials were turned to the page where Delta Dental had expressed the view that bleach kits submitted as occlusal guards were considered fraudulent. All my lawyers had done was deliver a weak opening statement—they hadn't even taken the floor to defend me—and now they were urging me to plea as if I had no chance. They were telling me I would probably have to plead guilty to at least two felony charges.

That evening, I drove in a daze to meet my parents. On the way, I phoned my brother Steve in Virginia to tell him the bad news. I couldn't believe this was happening.

"Holy shit, Buck," he said. "You've been fighting this crap for so long, over three years. It's just, it's absolutely insane. So, if you continue, and you lose, what will the government do?"

"Well," I replied, "it's pretty bad. I mean, I'm looking at a maximum of 122 years in prison for what they say I did."

"How fucking ridiculous is that! And that's how they can get you to plea out, by making the risk so absurd!"

"I've been dragged through the mud for so long," I said, "I just want to get back to my old life."

"So, you think your lawyers can get you off without prison time?" Steve said.

"No, it's all federal regulations and guidelines that decide how much prison time you have to do, depending on the severity of the crime. My lawyers think there'll be a significant fine, but they don't think I'll go to prison. That would be mad: prison, for the pennies they think I took."

"We should finish this," said Steve, decisively. "If you go to trial for a month and lose, you could go to jail for a very long time."

I reached my parents' house, where we talked it all out for several hours. My younger brother, Matt, was also there. My mom and dad had attended court, so they knew it wasn't looking good for me, but still they couldn't understand why my lawyers weren't motivated to defend me rather than settle.

"I don't know either, Mom," I said. "But today was really all government. Now it's about mitigating risk. Tomorrow those guys are supposed to defend me, but they told me if I were to plead out tomorrow before they started, the government would be far more inclined to accept a plea."

"What's the plea?" asked my mother.

"I will probably have to plea out to two felonies," I replied.

She lowered her head and placed her hands over her face. The sound of her muffled sobs filled the room.

After driving home I sat quietly in my car for a while praying to God. "Dear Lord, please help me make the right decision." I sat motionless, deep in thought, for around 40 minutes. Then I made my decision.

It was about 11 o'clock when I called Mr. Daniels to tell him I was prepared to cave. "Excellent news," he said. "So I'll need you to come into my office early tomorrow morning. We need to go over this because I'll have to speak to the prosecution before the proceedings start at 9:30 a.m. Then I'll need to meet with you again before we go into the courtroom. We'll make sure things work out the best we can for you here. You're making the right decision, Doc."

"So, what am I going to have to plead out to?"

"Two felonies. One insurance count and one IRS count."

"But what does that mean . . . for my future?"

"Well, most likely there's going to be an IRS penalty. They're saying all those credits or whatever they have, you probably owe about $80 grand in taxes. I don't know where they're getting their numbers—there's nothing to take it from—but that's what they have."

"What about the insurance?" I asked.

"Well, you'll probably have to pay back the insurance companies some money as well. I estimate a total of about $130,000 for the two counts."

"$130,000? Aren't we going to argue all of the work was done? And that if I owe an insurance company anything, it's for the sealant and maybe the occlusal guards alone?"

"Doc, you're right, but we'll need to make that argument later, not now."

"So if the restitution is all paid off before the sentencing, will that help me avoid the possibility of prison?"

"Doc, that's all up to the judge, but I seriously doubt you'll do any time. I'll meet with them and get this sorted out tomorrow."

"Okay, I can handle the financial part. I really don't care about the money. I just need to get past this so I can get back to my family, my practice, and normal life again. Thanks, I'll see you early tomorrow."

The Sixth Amendment guarantees that, "in all criminal prosecutions, the accused shall enjoy the right to a speedy and public trial, by an impartial jury." In practice, the vast majority of defendants in the United States are bullied and scared into plea-bargaining, myself included.

Writing in the *Washington Post* on May 20, 2020, Pulitzer Prize winning columnist George F. Will succinctly summarized how the plea-bargaining system has infected the entire US justice system and placed "intolerable pressure designed to induce a waiver" of the "fundamental right to a fair trial." Plea bargaining, he argued, is "pervasive and coercive" because of the trial penalty: "the difference between the sentences offered to those who plead guilty, and the much more severe sentences typically imposed after a trial . . . discourages exercising a constitutional right."

The article also drew attention to the prosecutors' routine practice of "piling on ('stacking') criminal charges to expose defendants to extreme sentences . . . can cause innocent people to plead guilty in order to avoid risking protracted incarceration for themselves..." and prolonged heartache for their loved ones.

That certainly was the situation in my case.

Will also lamented, "Such pressures effectively transfer sentencing power from judges to prosecutors." He then posed the million-dollar question: "How exactly are these pressures morally preferable to those that used to be administered by truncheons in the back of police stations?"

In 2014, Jed S. Rakoff, then a Senior US District Court judge, wrote a seminal essay entitled, "Why Innocent People Plead Guilty," which is essential reading for anyone wishing to understand how degraded the US justice system has become. It stated a shocking statistic, "In 2013, while 8 percent of all federal criminal charges were dismissed . . . more than 97 percent of the remainder were resolved through plea bargains, and fewer than 3 percent went to trial. The plea bargains largely determined the sentences imposed."

The situation is almost as bad at the state level. "It is a rare state where plea bargains do not similarly account for the resolution of at least 95 percent of the felony cases that are not dismissed . . . Furthermore, in both the state and federal systems, the power to determine the terms of the plea bargain is, as a practical matter, lodged largely in the prosecutor, with the defense counsel having little say and the judge even less."

That wasn't always the case, however. Plea bargains were rarely used until the crime rate rose sharply after the Civil War, and then plea bargaining seemed the ideal way to process defendants quickly while taking pressure off the courts. In those early days, it seemed like a win–win, despite reservations voiced at the time by the Supreme Court. Plea bargains encouraged defendants to cooperate with law enforcement to reduce their prison time, allowing the number of costly and time-consuming trials to be cut.

By the 1950s, plea bargains in the United States resolved more than 80 percent of all criminal cases, but there was no harsh penalty in place for those who chose to go to trial and were found guilty, so the system was still fit for purpose, plus the crime rate then was relatively low. In the subsequent three decades, crime soared, mostly due to illegal drugs and weapon crime, and so legislatures responded with a raft of harsh mandatory minimum sentences for the possession of even small quantities of drugs, including marijuana.

For weapons crime, if two weapons were involved, the second weapon alone brought a mandatory 25-year sentence on top of the 15-year sentence for the first weapon. Many of these sentences had to be imposed consecutively, rather than concurrently, so it wasn't long before defendants faced the threat of obligatory prison sentences of many decades to life, and the judges were powerless to intervene.

In 1984, Congress introduced "a regime of mandatory sentencing guidelines designed to avoid 'irrational' sentencing disparities." Since these guidelines "left judges with some limited discretion, it was not perceived at first how, perhaps even more than mandatory minimums, such a guidelines regime . . . transferred power over sentencing away from judges and into the hands of prosecutors."

As a result, between 1980 and 2010, the number of federal defendants going to trial dropped from 19 percent to just 3 percent, which is the current figure. The reason for this, as Rakoff points out, is that the mandatory sentencing guidelines "provide prosecutors with weapons to bludgeon defendants into effectively coerced plea bargains." Today, the United States has 5 percent of the world's total population, and yet it incarcerates 25 percent of all prisoners across the globe.

It was little wonder then that my attorney had his sights set on a plea bargain from the moment I retained him. He was an experienced and pragmatic defense attorney who knew one individual couldn't fix a broken system. It was his job, his duty even, to salvage the best outcome for his clients by working within those flawed and narrow parameters, rather than risk earning them a long prison sentence by making a futile stand to rock a boat that had already been comprehensively thwarted.

My precious liberty was doomed from the day I was indicted.

CHAPTER TWENTY-TWO

PLEA BARGAIN

"In many courts, plea bargaining serves the convenience of the judge and the lawyers, not the ends of justice."
- Jimmy Carter

After a sleepless night, I breathed in a deep lungful of crisp March air before climbing into my car to drive to Mr. Daniel's office to seal my fate. I briefly discussed the plea deal with Mr. Daniels and then he met with the prosecution. When the court was called to session, and the jury was led in to take their seats, both parties were called up to confer with the judge in a hushed huddle, as we have all seen in numerous legal dramas on television.

To the excitement of all the jurors, especially the truck driver, the judge announced the jury was to be dismissed, and a change of plea would be entered. It was a whopping, 17-page plea agreement, dated March 5, 2010, which I have extracted and inserted in Appendix A at the back of this book.

After listening to this entire agreement, I turned cold all over. I was playing the starring role in my own horror movie and horror movies never had happy endings.

My lawyers were packing up their things when I overheard Mr. Daniels talking with one of the prosecutors. They were shaking hands—in a way that looked like good sportsmanship—when I heard the prosecutor say, "Jeez Joel, that certainly took long enough."

I'm sure that was not something either one of them wanted me to hear, but that's when I lost all respect for our justice system.

Initially, my sentencing date was set for June 14, 2010, at 12:30 p.m. This was subsequently moved to July 19. So much, I thought, for a quick resolution.

I returned to work and buried myself in my patients' needs for the next four months. That whole summer was pretty much uneventful, although the approaching date for sentencing was constantly on my mind. I was in a state of limbo, feeling permanently anxious because of the uncertainty.

Meanwhile, my boys and I continued to carry on as if nothing was happening. We spent our annual week on Lake Anna, in Virginia, at the family boat house, spending time with the ones we love and camping with my parents along Lake Ontario. Our summers were always filled with trips and games around our own house and lots of boys' time. I swore that this year was going to be nothing different.

My lawyers had told me to expect a hefty fine and/or some kind of restitution to the various insurance companies that the government said I'd defrauded (although at no time did an insurance company go on record as saying it had been defrauded). I was working solidly and also coaching my lacrosse team as a valued member of the community—something my attorney had leveraged during his rather weak opening statement back in March.

Everyone in Newfane knew something was going down with me. I had pled guilty, so I felt everyone, including those kids on the lacrosse team, must have presumed I was guilty. After all, I'd made such a big deal of saying I was innocent and that I intended to fight to the bitter end to clear my name. Once I pled out, some people took the view that not only had I been guilty all along but also I had made things worse by pretending to be innocent. As a result, I suddenly switched from being innocent to being guilty and pernicious for lying about it.

I remember in particular that, before the plea, I'd been interviewed by a journalist about the case, and he'd written a sympathetic article that presented me as a wronged family man. After the plea, when we crossed paths again, he accused me of manipulating him, of cynically feeding him a line about my innocence.

Some people around town started to act differently around me, and I can understand why. We all assume innocent people don't plead guilty, but they didn't know I was facing a maximum sentence of 122 years in prison, and they were unaware of the circumstances of the case. Those few months waiting for my sentence were humbling, to say the least.

I didn't make any contingency plans for my dental practice in the unlikely event I would be sent to prison. Even though a prison sentence was technically possible, as set out by the federal guidelines in the plea agreement, my lawyers hoped there would be no prison time. They figured the judge would take into account my lack of criminal history and give me a second chance. One of my lawyers, George Muscato, spoke to the press a week before sentencing, and it was actually printed in the newspaper that he believed I would do no time.

I was swept along by this fantasy, as I had been told to expect only to pay some hefty fines and restitution, and how could I do that if I was stuck in prison, rather than working? I think I also reasoned that having two felonies against my name, even though I was innocent, was embarrassing and shameful enough, without the added injustice of prison. Things were already so bad that surely I'd seen all my bad luck by now.

It's clear to me now I was engaging in a type of cognitive distortion that psychologists call "minimization"—refusing to fully confront the negative consequences of my behavior. I also received so many letters of support and character references from businesspeople, politicians, teachers, clergy, and even the local senator, that I was convinced the judge would see my innate goodness.

And I did something further. I actually believed the judge would see my innocence, since who better to appreciate the unjust nature of a broken plea-bargaining system than a federal judge? During the three days of trial, before my plea bargain, Judge Arcara had appeared stern but fair. On several occasions, I had spotted him frowning as he concentrated on the prosecution's case, and the only time I had seen him become impatient was with the government attorney. So I somehow managed to convince myself that, if anything, the judge was erring on my side. This was another example of my delusional thinking.

On July 19, 2010, the day of the sentencing, the court was filled with my family and friends—a show of force designed to sway the judge into preserving my precious liberty. My attorney, Mr. Daniels, stood up and said a few words on my behalf, which followed his usual "pillar-of-the-community" argument—that I had built a big, beautiful office in Newfane that also offered community facilities, that I was a good dentist, and I coached a lacrosse team in my free time.

When Judge Arcara addressed the court, it was immediately apparent he thought a lot less of me than I had allowed myself to believe. "Mr. Daniels, obviously this man was held in high regard by his community. I have read every single one of his testimonial letters—I have never seen so many—but I assure you, that last night I read each one carefully. I have struggled to understand why someone in his position would do this. *The only explanation that makes sense is pure greed. Dr. Geise must be an exceptionally greedy man.*"

And then he turned to look directly at me.

"Dr. Geise, do you have anything to say?"

"Your honor," I replied, "I have given the shirt off my back to everyone around me. I'm not greedy. I've tried to do everything possible for the people in my community. Everything. If anything, I'm guilty of being too generous."

With that, Judge Arcara said, "I will take a short recess and spend some time in my chambers and then I will return with my decision."

Fifteen minutes later, Judge Arcara came back to the courtroom. Even with all the amazing letters of heartfelt support my peers had written to the court, both earnest and consistent for me as a person, nothing could persuade the court system to open its eyes and finally see the charges against me were totally unsubstantiated.

"Well, I have reached a decision. I sentence Dr. Geise

to 15 months in prison for each of Counts 3 and 63, to be served concurrently, with the supervised release of three years (Count 3) and 1 year (Count 63) to be served concurrently."

There was an immediate hush in the courtroom, then first some quiet crying from the people behind me and then louder cries with outright gestures of frustration.

Further, "I order him to pay the insurance companies he defrauded in the amount of $40,022.85 and to the Internal Revenue Service in the amount of $87,781.97. I am mindful of the importance of a deterrent in this case. Without a prison sentence, where is the deterrent to keep someone else from committing the same fraud as Dr. Geise?"

All Mr. Daniels could put together at that point was, "I understand. Thank you, your honor."

I was in total shock now. I scanned the courtroom and spotted many people in tears, including both of my parents, who were in the front row. There was now a room full of people crying and shaking their heads, with anger in their eyes, so I started walking toward my mother to hug her, when a reporter shoved a microphone in my face and asked, "Dr. Geise, now what are your plans?"

I just looked at her and shook my head in disgust. How insensitive could someone possibly be?

I carried on walking and went to comfort my mom and dad, who were absolutely crushed. I wasn't dragged off to prison immediately by two burly guards, like on television. I was never handcuffed throughout the entire nightmare. Instead, I was allowed to walk out of the courtroom to commiserate with the people who'd given me their support.

Another court date was set to determine where and when I would be required to surrender myself to the Bureau of Prisons. I'd already had my fingerprints taken on the day of the plea, and it was curious, as I went home still a free man. It was beyond surreal.

CHAPTER TWENTY-THREE

INCARCERATION

"We have a racially based justice system that over punishes, fails to rehabilitate, and doesn't make us safer."

- Piper Kerman

The facility selected for me was a medium-security federal prison for male inmates called the Federal Correctional Institution, McKean (FCI McKean), in northern Pennsylvania. I would be placed in the adjacent satellite prison camp, which houses minimum-security male offenders. McKean is located about a two-and-a-half-hour drive south of my home in Newfane.

Before I was scheduled to go there, my attorneys arranged for me to meet an ex-inmate (who also just happened to be an attorney), so he could tell me what to expect. He told me to be ready for an exercise in boredom because it was going to be Groundhog Day every single day. He told me I would have to find something to occupy my time. He also noted the prisoners were mostly racially segregated and didn't mix.

I was also put in touch with a guy who was still serving time. We exchanged a few emails; he gave me some advice, and I think he pulled a few strings to make sure I wouldn't get bunked in with anyone dangerous.

Anyway, that preparation was all for nothing because a week before my prison sentence began, I was notified I would be going instead to Canaan Prison in Pennsylvania, 20 miles northeast of Scranton and over *five hours* away from Newfane. Presumably just to stick it to me even more, they just made it exceptionally harder for my family and friends to visit me. Canaan was a high-security penitentiary, with a satellite unit for minimum-security prisoners like me.

Other than that, I knew nothing about it. I had no insider knowledge whatsoever. Meanwhile, the local newspapers were having a ball reporting my demise. The FBI issued a press release, which I have printed here in full as it makes for stark (and devastating) reading:

~

"Dentist Sentenced to 15 Months in Prison for Filing a False Health Care Claim and Filing a False Tax Return

U.S. Attorney's Office
July 19, 2010
Western District of New York (716) 843-5700

BUFFALO, NY—U.S. Attorney William J. Hochul, Jr. announced today that Scott D. Geise, 48, a practicing dentist from Newfane, New York, was sentenced to 15 months in prison and three years' supervised release by U.S. District Judge Richard J. Arcara after pleading guilty to filing a false health care claim and filing a false tax return. Geise's trial had already begun with witnesses being called when he decided to take a plea. Also, as part of his sentence, Judge Arcara also ordered Geise to pay restitution in the amount of $40,022.85 to the insurance companies that he defrauded and $87,781.97 to the Internal Revenue Service for taxes owed.

Assistant U.S. Attorneys Timothy C. Lynch and John E. Rogowski, who handled the case, stated that the defendant admitted to devising a scheme to defraud insurance companies by submitting false claim forms to, and receiving unearned payments from, the insurance companies. For instance, when certain patients asked for a bleach whitening kit, which was not covered by insurance, the defendant and/or the defendant's employees would instead bill the patient's insurance company for an occlusal guard, which was covered.

AUSA's Lynch and Rogowski further stated that the defendant admitted to employing an additional scheme to defraud General Motors' and Delphi's self-insured dental insurance plan by billing the insurance plan for placing amalgams (silver fillings) in the teeth of several patients, when in fact, the defendant simply applied sealants on the teeth of the patients. The insurance plan did not cover sealants but did cover amalgams.

As part of the plea agreement, the defendant also admitted to assisting another person with submitting a fraudulent claim for health care benefits to the Laborers Local 91 Welfare Fund.

Geise also admitted to filing a false tax return. He admitted that he failed to record cash receipts for his business, Newfane Family Dentistry, P.C., as income, therefore, the corporate tax returns from 2003 to 2005 failed to list over $188,000 in income and the defendant failed to pay corporate taxes of $58,254. Geise also failed to pay taxes on his personal returns for the years 2002 through 2005 in the amount of $29,527.

In this time of rising health care costs and premiums, health care fraud is something my office will not tolerate on any level" said U.S. Attorney Hochul. "When the health care system is defrauded, it drives up costs for everyone, especially those who can least afford it."

The investigation was the culmination of an investigation of special agents of the Department of Labor, Office of Inspector General, under the direction of Marjorie Franzman, Special Agent in Charge; the Federal Bureau of Investigation, under the direction of James Robertson, Special Agent in Charge; the Internal Revenue Service, under the direction of Charles Pine, Special Agent in Charge; the Niagara County Sheriff's Department, under the direction of Sheriff James Voutour, and the District's Health Care Fraud Task Force."

~

Even at this stage, I tried to remain optimistic. I was thinking of prison time as an unpleasant blip, much like a military deployment that I needed to get through, and then I could return to my three boys, my dental practice, and the rest of my life.

How wrong I was.

It would take me years to get my life and dental career back. I didn't know then that prison was just the beginning of a new and difficult phase of my life and by no means the end of my troubles.

I had to leave Newfane on September 18, 2010, a

gorgeous and sunny Saturday afternoon during the JV football season. My son Stone was playing that day. I was there with my parents and my girlfriend, Larina. My ex-wife was also there and made sure Myles and Thorne were there for me as well. We just enjoyed the day, all together, sitting in the bleachers.

I watched Stone play most of his football game, but we all knew I had to leave before the end of the game, while he was still on the field. So the coach, knowing Stone wasn't going to see me for a year, let him out of the game for a while. He took off his helmet, and he was kneeling at the end of a line of boys as we all started walking toward my parents' van.

I was halfway around the track when I stopped to wave back at him, to say goodbye. That was incredibly hard to do. What goes through a kid's mind when he's watching his dad walk off to prison? He gave me a wave back in solidarity, but I could see the pain in his face from 50 yards away. That is a visual I will never, ever forget.

We all met at the van for a few minutes while we waited for my nieces and nephews who had come to say their tearful goodbyes to "Uncle Buck."

But now it was time to go. That Saturday afternoon, my parents drove Larina and me to Scranton, and we all spent my final night of freedom in a hotel there, drinking beer from the cooler Dad had brought, and reminiscing. We just hung out. It was a very precious evening.

The next morning, we got up, and my parents took us out for breakfast. We pulled over when we saw a diner called "Bucks," ironically, and ordered pancakes and sausages. The meal sat heavily in my stomach as we climbed back in the van and set off for the prison. I was driving and gripped the wheel harder than usual as I had to use the GPS because we were in the middle of nowhere, and the older GPS just wasn't as accurate as it is today. It was the most anxious drive of my life.

Eventually, we ended up at an austere, multistory facility surrounded by barbed wire. It looked like the mental institution from *One Flew over the Cuckoo's Nest.* I pulled in through what looked like the main gate, and I spoke to one of the guards. "Hi, my name's Scott Geise, and I'm here to self-surrender."

The guard frowned, "I'm sorry, would you repeat that?"

As I was beginning to tell him again, he said, "You must be looking for Canaan," and he directed me around the facility and back onto the same street again toward Canaan. That was a common problem with early GPS, which routed into, instead of around, wrong destinations. I was praying this wouldn't make us late and breathed a sigh of relief when I finally spotted a sign that said CANAAN PRISON CAMP. Once again, we pulled into the parking lot, and just as I was getting out of the car, a huge guy lumbered over waving his arms.

"You can't self-surrender here, you're in the wrong place. Right place, wrong building."

He then directed me up the hill to the main building, and I later discovered the lumbering man was the warden of the prison camp.

I set off once again and drove up the hill to an official-looking administrative building, and at least there I could see some activity. Once again, there was no clear signage. My heart was hammering hard against my ribs. I didn't want to be late, but I was also experiencing a jarring sense of relief because I realized I'd finally reached the correct place. Despite all the detours, we were about a half-hour early.

I introduced myself yet again and the attendee asked us to take a seat, as they weren't quite ready to process me yet. So the four of us sat silently, all holding hands in a row—Dad, Mom, myself, and Larina—all trying not to burst into tears. Waiting. And waiting. My senses were by now on overdrive. This was a new and potentially hostile environment, so I was alert, combing the surroundings, and aware of the slightest noise or movement. The odor of carbolic disinfectant burned in my nostrils. Then I spotted a guy sweeping and collecting garbage. Our eyes met a couple of times; he would then glance over to the desk, then back to me, and then he vanished. I didn't know whether he was a prisoner or an employee. What were the social rules here?

Finally, a guard walked over and called me up to the front desk to start the checking-in procedure. It was time to say goodbye. My girlfriend was very concerned to make sure I had enough money in my prison account. No money changed hands inside the prison, so, to be able to buy toothpaste or soap or whatever, it was all done by quoting your account number. We had been told to bring cash so we could open the account, but here at the prison they told us they didn't accept cash, so Larina would now have to find another way to provide me with the funds I would require even just for basic needs.

They left me at the counter, and it took all my effort to keep standing tall. I couldn't bear to watch my family as they limped back to the parking lot. I kept my eyes on the life ahead of me instead, paying careful attention to what the officer was saying to me. I was on my own and utterly clueless about what to expect—a complete and utter blank canvas. I didn't know anything, and I didn't know what I didn't know. It was very unnerving, having nothing to contextualize my surroundings except what I'd read in books or seen dramatized on television.

I was hyper-alert, but I tried to stay calm by taking some deep breaths. Finally, the guard walked over and said, "Follow me. We're going to walk through a portal over there, but before we get there, I'm going to need to frisk you, to make sure you're not hiding anything."

"Yes sir," I replied. "I'm certainly not hiding anything."

I put my hands over my head, and he patted me down and then had me put my hands behind my back. I was being handcuffed for the first time in my life.

"We're going to walk forward here, and I'll be guiding you through this whole process until we can get you in," the officer told me.

He was a white guy in his forties. Very polite, very affable. And then he said, "So, you're a dentist, huh?" I nodded and said yes, and he said, "Hmm, that's interesting."

This was just a casual conversation, but, in these strange surroundings, it was tempting to over-analyze everything, because I still didn't know the rules. For all I knew, I was being too familiar with the guards. Maybe I had already given away too much information. Or maybe he was just a regular guy trying to put me at ease.

"I doubt anyone in here is going to call you Doc," he said. "The guards will use your surname."

By this time, we'd reached a glass partition. The guard

gave his number and his name.

"State your name," said the guard on the other side of the glass, referring to me.

"Scott Geise."

We were buzzed through into a chamber big enough for about 30 people. The door closed behind us, and I had to walk over to another window and say my name to get buzzed into the next chamber. Then I walked out through a door into blinding sunlight, onto a strip of dirt and a narrow track that ran around the massive walled facility, bordered on either side by 12-foot-high glimmering concertina wire.

We worked our way across this cinder track for another 15 yards to get to the next door, which took me back inside the wall to another cubicle area. This was the big facility, the maximum-security prison, where guys were doing multiple life sentences for murder.

I was led into a processing room, where I was frisked again. Then I had to strip naked and perform a degrading squat to make sure I wasn't carrying anything in my butt cheeks. The guard checked inside my mouth and then gave me a pair of badly-fitting, size-16 army boots and my prison clothes—brown army underwear, brown T-shirt, and a green uniform that was three sizes too big.

It would have fit a 350-pound, 6' 8" NFL lineman. I had to roll the legs up several times over, and I sat there for what seemed like hours until finally, the guards returned to escort me back to the in-processing facility.

So I had to retrace my steps—into the sunlight, through the concertina wire corridor, and the lock chamber—until I was back in the place where I had said goodbye to Larina and my parents. I was instructed to sit in the same chair while I waited for the van that would shuttle me to my quarters.

When the van pulled up, I was told to walk out and sit in the passenger seat next to the driver, who was obviously also a prisoner. He didn't say much as I got in, nothing more than a quick hello. The van then drove back down the hill to another facility, where he stopped to let four prisoners climb in the back. They knew I was a new inmate, so I think they made a point of being loud, just to make me feel unnerved.

One of the guys was called "Fiddy," as in 50 Cent, the rapper. He started calling out to me, so I turned around and caught his eye. We proceeded to stare each other down. Fiddy continued to verbally harass me, and then he said,

"Tough guy, huh? Shit, you about to be introduced to a whole new world."

So I turned back around to face the front and didn't say a word. The driver looked at me and nodded, smiling. He was enjoying the banter. I later discovered he and Fiddy were bunkmates.

We reached the camp, and the other guys jumped out the sliding door and walked off to do whatever they had to do. To my relief, they weren't interested in picking a fight with me. The driver then pointed out the warden's office and instructed me to head over to it. When I entered, I was told to sit in one of the chairs. The warden then introduced himself and let me know how the camp was run, how and when to get my inmate clothing, when the meals were served, and some other general information.

He finished up by giving me his stock advice: "Don't

accept anything from anyone and don't give anything to anyone. Just follow the rules, and we'll have no problems, and you'll do just fine. Here's your bedding. Your bunkie is Mike N. Another inmate will be here in a moment to take you there."

As if on cue, a young Italian guy appeared. He had such thick dark eyelashes, that I thought he was wearing mascara, and I'd stumbled into some kind of *Kiss of the Spider Woman* scenario. It turned out he simply happened to have naturally thick eyelashes. No subtext. I was still overthinking everything. As he walked me to my bunk, he asked, "So is it true you're a dentist?"

"How does everybody know this already?" I said.

"Oh, word travels fast in the prison. Like, the smallest thing. You know, there are only 148 of us. News gets around."

When we reached the barracks building, a wide-open room that housed 75 double bunks, we walked down the third aisle and reached the third set of bunks; I was told the one on the left was mine. My bunkie introduced himself as "White Mike," which seemed an unusual name until the black guy on the other side of the aisle leaned over and said, "And I'm Black Mike."

White Mike made sure to point out he had the bottom bunk, and I had the top bunk. The bottom bunk is preferable because it means you don't have to climb up and down all the time; you can just sit down at the desk and locker across. I didn't have a problem either way, and I was just putting my bedding onto my bunk when another inmate introduced himself.

"Hi, I'm Newburg. I came in yesterday."

"I'm sorry to hear that. I'm Scott Geise. Good to meet

you."

Surreal.

Then I noticed people were starting to leave their bunks and wander out of the barracks. White Mike explained it was nearly time for lunch. He said he was going to head over to the chow line, but he'd be back soon.

Then another guy came over. He was holding a clear plastic bag that contained a pair of shower shoes. "Take them," he said, staring at the floor as he pressed the bag furtively against my arm. "Better than your oversized army boots. More comfortable."

Just moments ago, I'd been told Rule Number One: don't accept anything from another prisoner. I looked around and could see everyone else had sneakers and T-shirts and no one was wearing their army boots.

"Take them," he urged. "No joke. You'll need them for the shower. I wouldn't even think about stepping in there without them, and you can't buy any yet. You'll get a new uniform tomorrow when everyone goes to work. They just give you this crappy shit to wear on the first day."

I'd been here less than an hour, and already I faced a dilemma. Then a second, shorter, very clean-cut Middle Eastern looking guy with glasses chipped in. "Hey, man, don't sweat it. We all just wear what's comfortable, so you'll be happier in those shower shoes."

"Yeah, they gave them to me, too," said Newburg. "It's no big deal."

Reluctantly, I took off my army boots and accepted the shower shoes. Did this mean I was in debt to him now? Would he try to extort a crazy price when my money came through? Or was he just being helpful? I didn't know.

I mulled this over as I joined the lunch line. Then I spotted a huge inmate with long hair and a rough-looking scowl, who seemed to be staring at me. *Now what?* He looked at my feet and shook his head slightly, still scowling, like Lurch from the Adam's Family. Something was up. I didn't know what, but I was about to find out.

I reached for a pile of trays, picked one up, and shuffled along to get some food. Then I looked over at a guard who was staring at me and pointing aggressively at the floor in front of him, which was the universal sign language for, "Get your ass over here, right now." I put the tray down and double-timed it over to him.

"Yes, sir," I said.

"Geise," said the guard, rolling his eyes. "I know you're new. I get that it's your first day. But do not, and I say, do not EVER come into MY cafeteria wearing those goddam shower shoes again, you understand? Now, get back to your bunk and put your boots on."

I was an idiot, hazed before I'd even eaten my first meal. I rushed back to change into my boots and rejoined the back of the chow line, kicking myself for being so stupid. I sat and ate alone, feeling very conspicuous in my oversized uniform and ill-fitting boots.

The next morning, everyone headed off to work, and I had to join a group of newbies to meet with the head guard and get assigned a job. He was a small, fat, arrogant guy who treated us all with thinly concealed contempt. It seemed he was fond of barking orders, swearing, and reminding us he was in charge.

A little dog with a big bark, he was close to retirement, so he was just serving his time, looking forward to the moment when he could get out of this hell hole once and for all.

He was also the guy who assigned all the jobs, so he took great pleasure in telling us there was an assortment of jobs around the camp we could apply for, but that most of us would be landscaping: "Guys that have been here longer, get priority, but you newbies, you're going to do anything I fucking say you're going to do." He was that crass with everything. He took every opportunity to demonstrate his unsuitability for leadership.

"Right. So, before I finish. Has anyone got any physical problems? Any restrictions?"

Here was my opportunity to attract ridicule, once again, but I decided to speak up anyway. "Yes, sir. I'll work any job here, but I have two herniated discs in my lower back, so heavy lifting could be a problem."

I fully expected him to laugh and swear and ridicule me in front of the other guys, but he just raised an eyebrow and nodded, no doubt filing away that bit of information in his tiny brain so he could exploit it later. Then he continued. "The good news is you new fish all get to do landscaping. You'll be filling sandbags outside in the fresh air. You might even have to lift some sandbags. If that's alright with you, Ms. Geise?"

I spent the next three months filling sandbags.

Later that week I received the standard issue of three sets of uniforms, all in my size, one of which was strictly reserved for meeting visitors, so at least I could fall into somewhat of a routine. After a few weeks, I began to realize that despite my initial fears I was fairly safe.

Most of the guards were reasonable, and no prisoner could be admitted to the facility if they had been convicted of anything violent, or for using a weapon. Nobody was here for those types of crimes, or, if they were, they'd already spent 10 years showing good behavior. Plus, no one wanted to go to a rougher, high-security prison, so it was in everyone's interest to do their time and stay out of each other's faces.

Only about 25 percent of the guys were white, with the other three-quarters being Black, Asian, Middle Eastern, or Hispanic. Most were imprisoned for minor drug-related offenses, and the others were white-collar crimes. I didn't know about individual crimes, as it was an unwritten rule you never asked. Someone could choose to tell you if he wanted to, but most kept quiet about what they'd done, especially the white-collar guys. You'd hear rumors about certain prisoners, but that was all.

We were counted five times every 24 hours—just before chow line in the morning then at lunchtime then evening then twice during the middle of the night. The guards would walk through the bunks with flashlights while we slept. There were no walls around the Prison Camp, so frequent counting was absolutely necessary. Everyone was known either by their last name or by a nickname like Detroit (because a guy was from Detroit). It was pretty basic, but despite what the guard had told me, everyone called me "Doc", even the guards after they got to know me.

We were paid for the work we did, especially because we had to buy most of our basic supplies for staying clean and washing our clothes. Short-stay prisoners received 9 cents an hour as their wage or 72 cents a day for eight hours; guys who had been there longer received 14 cents an hour, and they were at the top of the salary ladder.

We were a large, dirt-cheap workforce—150 men paid the equivalent of one minimum wage employee—and all the jobs were focused on maintaining the prison buildings and the surrounding real estate. Of course, that business model collapses without a steady supply of prisoners, so it's important to keep the prisons full of cheap labor.

Every morning, shortly after the breakfast line finished, I boarded a bus with about 50 other inmates, and we were taken on a half-mile ride up to the maintenance and utility buildings. "G Ward," the one and only bus driver, would roll out of the camp and step on the pedal to defy gravity as he attempted to take the left hairpin turn a little faster than he did the previous time. The guys just knew to lean away from the turn when the bus got closer. It was a little unnerving at first, but every time he dropped us all off I thanked him for getting us there safely, whether it was to or from work. G Ward would just smile.

The grounds were extensive, so lots of prisoners had to weed whack, mow grass, and pick up leaves. Day after day we filled those sandbags, loaded them onto pallets, and a forklift took them away. It was repetitive, boring, and physically exhausting.

One day, one of the officers came over, looking for volunteers. He asked if any of us were sick of filling sandbags and were curious to know where they all went. I didn't care if it was a trick question; I said I'd love to try something different. I and about six other guys were taken over to the guard's firing range. The sandbags were needed to rebuild the area behind the targets, which badly needed remodeling, as it had been completely shot to pieces. Our new assignment was to build a series of bullet traps on the hill behind the targets.

One of the guys set up the first row cockeyed, so when we built up the next rows of sandbags, it looked a mess, and we were told to start all over again. I hate having to redo anything, so I try to make sure, no matter what the task is at hand, that it is done right the first time. How you do anything is how you do everything! This time I took charge and lined up a foundation row of sandbags that were perfectly straight and even. It must have brought out the dentist in me! The line was so good the guard officially put me in charge so every trap we built could achieve the same quality. That was how I ended up spending the next month and a half building sandbag bullet traps for the guards to practice on.

But, to me, it was simply a project worth doing, something productive, and it took my mind off all the things that could be going on at home. I missed my boys, my family, and my girlfriend more than you could possibly imagine.

CHAPTER TWENTY-FOUR

PARTNERS IN CRIME

"It takes two flints to make a fire."

- Louisa May Alcott

One day, as we were stacking our sandbags around, one of the guys said to me, "Hey, Doc, did you know there's another dentist in here?"

"Another dentist? No, I didn't know. Who is he?"

"His name is Stradford. He works in the power plant where all the heating, air conditioning, water, all that shit is done."

"Why haven't I met him?"

"He works the night shift—that's probably why."

I was intrigued to meet this other dentist, if not to just talk dentistry again but to find out what he had been doing to keep his sanity in this place. It wasn't long before I finally got to meet Stradford after my bunkie, White Mike, pointed him out to me one afternoon in the chow line.

We hit it off immediately, and he asked me where they had me working. I told him I was on the firing range, and he said the guy he was working with at the power plant was about to go home on appeal, so there would soon be a vacancy. The only difference was that the work hours were offset with the rest of the inmates.

I talked to the guard in charge, asking if the job was available, and, most likely due to my background in science, he transferred me from landscaping the next day. Working the night shift was a godsend because it kept me away from the chaos and busyness of the rest of the prison. It also meant that, after I'd grabbed some sleep, I had the whole facility to myself during the daytime. I could monopolize the computer room while everyone else was out working, avoiding the busy time in the evening when everyone else wanted to send emails.

Night shift in the power plant was an easy gig. First, there was no manual labor involved. We spent some of the time performing tests on the water or making sure the heating was set correctly and the air conditioning was running smoothly, but the rest of the night was our own. There was plenty of time to hang out with Dr. Stradford and talk. We even had our own desks, so if we had personal stuff to do, such as work on our appeals, we could get on with it in peace.

We talked endlessly and became a team of sorts. He will always be a great friend of mine, and we stay in touch; I was even fortunate enough to attend his wedding. And not so surprisingly, there are lots of questionable details surrounding his conviction, just like mine. He'd been sentenced to six years for mail fraud and railroaded through the system with plenty of things happening during his trial that didn't add up. So we both started working on our appeals together. My girlfriend (now wife) was a paralegal, so she would send me information about my case. She even got ahold of my docket, which itemized everything from the indictment onwards in date order.

During the quiet time of the day, Stradford and I spent hours on the prison computer—what they called the law computer—without being disturbed, looking up precedents and reverse engineering the rulings of various judges to see if the correct procedure was followed in our trials. When judges and lawyers win cases, they gloat and talk about why they won; this reveals lots of procedural and technical information.

So, for example, a prosecutor might have won a case because of something a defense attorney failed to do. Or they won a case for one reason and the next case for a contradictory reason. It makes a mockery of the rules. We studied all these other cases and were able to figure out what our attorneys should have done in our cases to follow the correct procedures. It was a revelation because it turned out that, not only did our attorneys fail to do certain things, but the prosecutors also broke the rules on several occasions (such as signing *seven* continuous orders on *the same day)*.

It's important to note here that the government has to abide by the Speedy Trial Clock, making sure they bring a defendant to trial in a timely manner, and, if they're unable to do that, they lose their case. I spent a lot of time studying all the occasions other prosecutors had been able to pause the clock, and each time there had to be a good reason because the Speedy Trial Act was enacted simply to keep things fair for the accused and preserve the interests of justice.

So, whenever there needs to be a stoppage of that clock, the judge, defense attorneys, and prosecution have to agree before the continuance is signed. All parties must agree to stop the clock for a limited time while one or both sides are waiting to receive an important piece of information, or whatever, but then the remainder of the countdown continues.

When I looked at my docket, I was amazed to discover that, in my case, *seven* continuous orders had been signed on *the same day*. The government knew they had abused the clock, so they tried to get all the paperwork up to date in one quick deed. This was just before my first scheduled trial date in 2009. This was fraudulent. Clearly, there's one rule for the establishment and another for the rest of us.

This problem of the establishment breaking the law, to enforce it, is nothing new. This deep-seated issue hasn't just appeared overnight; it has been blighting our justice system and eroding the US Constitution for decades. Entire books have been written on the subject, such as *Constitutional Chaos: What Happens When the Government Breaks Its Own Laws* by the columnist and senior judicial analyst for Fox News, Judge Andrew P. Napolitano.

Published in 2006, the book opened with a chilling paragraph. "It should be against the law to break the law. Unfortunately, it is not. In early twenty-first century America, a long-standing dirty little secret still exists among public officials, politicians, judges, prosecutors, and police. The government—federal, state, and local—is not bound to obey its own laws."

The book was simply written and accessible, but Napolitano's forensic analysis of how those in power routinely broke the law made for uncomfortable reading, especially if, like me, you've been on the receiving end.

William L. Anderson, professor of economics at

Frostburg State University, summed up the book with this succinct précis, "Napolitano proceeds to demonstrate how government officials at all levels routinely violate the law, commit felonies, lie, use torture and other illegal methods to extract confessions from innocent people and generally act in a manner so cynical as to destroy the confidence that any of us could have in the law."

By January 2011, I'd already been in correspondence with my lawyers for some time. They made lots of empty promises about visiting me, but, beyond that, they remained characteristically uninvolved. However, their attitude changed completely the moment I requested a copy of my grand jury transcripts. They stopped communicating with me at that point, and I never heard from them again. It was as if they had dropped off the planet.

I never managed to get ahold of a copy of those grand jury transcripts. To me, it was a huge red flag that my lawyers wouldn't send them to me. This told me they'd overlooked something in my trial; they had either made a big mistake or failed to do something they plainly didn't want me to discover.

Undeterred, I kept working on my appeal. Rereading my docket, I started to suspect my superseding indictment had not been acquired legally. I didn't have any proof for this, but I had a hunch the prosecutors were so fixated on my pleading out that they failed to follow the proper procedure—something my lawyers should have picked up on.

I also looked into my right to a speedy trial. It had taken 32 long, torturous months to bring me to trial. But, every time there was a delay, the prosecutors wrote into the documentation (printed in full in Exhibit B of the government's answer to my 2255 appeal document) wording that concluded, "The Court further finds that as of January 10th, 2010, zero days of Speedy Trial Act time will have elapsed in this action and 70 days remain in the period within which defendant must be tried."

In the preceding 30 months, not a single day of speedy trial protection ticked off of that clock. They reset the clock each time, and, by the time the trial finally rolled around on March 3, 2010, the government claimed only 23 days had actually tolled. Was this legal? It's my understanding the government has a responsibility to make sure you're brought to trial correctly and speedily; otherwise, they lose their right to proceed against you.

And for good reason. The accused is in this position because the government says it has something on them, and the prosecutor shouldn't be allowed to stall the system when they don't have sufficient proof and keep the accused on the hook until they do find something.

During my studies of case law in prison, I even dug up an old case concerning a dentist from Buffalo, called Oberoi. He'd managed to get his conviction overturned in the Supreme Court because he was able to prove the continuances had not been duly agreed upon by the judge, defense counsel, and prosecution. He was able to show the prosecution had failed to follow the correct procedure.

The District Court judge, in that case, had even written a long explanation of how the system for continuances was supposed to work, and he explicitly stated you cannot backdate those continuance orders. You cannot delay the Speedy Trial Clock after the time has already passed, and there's a term for it—*nunc pro tunc*. The judge was none other than Judge Richard Arcara, the same man who judged my trial, and yet he had allowed seven backdated continuance orders to be signed on one day during my case.

Remember, it was the government who chose to abandon Count 1 after I was able to show the Fazzolaris had been fraudulently extracting precise amounts from their union fund for years and magically leaving the minimum balance of $1,000 each time. I was also able to show the crime indicted on me was a crime *specifically* intended for the *administrators* of the Local 91 Welfare Fund, and I had nothing to do with the union.

That had been the central pillar of their entire case against me, but when that collapsed, they simply tacked on another bunch of charges, Counts 2 through 65. The government was allowed to pursue those charges, after severance, without presenting them as an individual group to a grand jury. The judge should have known that was illegal. My lawyers should have known that was illegal. But those documents, at that juncture, had all been sealed, so everything involving the abandonment of Count 1, with all its flaws and procedural anomalies, was effectively buried.

I don't know the contents of those sealed documents, but I'm sure they're hiding important information that could have helped get my case dismissed before it reached trial. If anything, I would have been able to use that information when I took my case to the Appellate Court, but, to do that, my lawyers would have had to object to the way the case was being handled, and they never once did that. To this day, I still wonder why they ignored my request for a copy of the grand jury transcripts and went totally AWOL.

Undeterred, Dr. Stradford and I continued to spend every day in prison working on our appeals. In April 2011, I filed Motion 2255, which is the statutory vehicle a federal prisoner can use to mount a collateral attack on their conviction or sentence.

I was now forced to fight for myself. I sought to have my conviction vacated "based on a claim of ineffective assistance of counsel, in that the performance of his counsel, Joel L. Daniels and George V.C. Muscato, was deficient in that they recommended the petitioner plead guilty rather than to pursue a dismissal of the Superseding Indictment based on (1) a statute of limitations violation, and (2) a Speedy Trial Act violation."

The motion was denied. The judgment of the court was based upon the government's answer, which is indicative of the extent of decay within the system, and it was full of inaccuracies. They ignore such details as the correct length of my sentence, just regurgitating legal jargon, and this is all reproduced in Appendix B.

A month before my release, I filed a pro se appeal in July 2011, but it was denied on the grounds an appeal can only be granted if the defense team raises objections during the trial. As previously stated, my defense attorneys hadn't raised a single objection, so my appeal fell at the first hurdle.

Even after Count 1 was avoided and sealed, and the prosecution focused on other counts, my lawyers did not object, not even just to "create a record" and have an objection preserved in the future. They failed to perform even this simple duty, to create a legal backstop, which I have since learned is what all good trial lawyers routinely do to give their clients the possibility of appeal.

Stradford and I worked so hard that we attracted the attention of the other prisoners, who were naturally curious as to why we were always studying and carrying around papers and files. We'd frequently get asked if we were studying for a degree. Nobody bullied us or got up in our grill about it, either. Quite the opposite: they respected our diligence. Moreover, I also did my best to use my medical knowledge to help people if they needed it. When I had family visits, I would often have relatives of other inmates coming over to thank me for helping their loved ones.

There was an infirmary, but the doctor was borderline incompetent—and I'm not sure he had the prisoner's best interests in mind. He used to dish out so much medication it was not uncommon for a prisoner to fall over and bash his head because he was so dizzy and drugged up on prescription medication. Of course, as soon as a prison guard saw an injured prisoner, he'd assume he'd been in a fight, so that was another issue that needed careful handling, especially if I found myself first on the scene.

During those long hours, Dr. Stradford and I spent together, night after night in the power plant, with lots of time on our hands, we weren't playing cards or wasting our time shooting the breeze. We were working hard: researching our appeals and devising an ambitious plan to overhaul the entire healthcare system in the United States. What else do you do in prison? With our combined expertise and experience, we began to figure out a way to optimize the delivery of health care.

It was a simple but formidable plan that aimed to facilitate and prioritize deep cooperation between various medical healthcare professionals to improve communication, eliminate duplication, and improve efficiency. The idea was to link dental and medical services together when a patient is first examined. The collaboration between these two frontline healthcare professionals would lead to a more accurate diagnosis and more efficient holistic treatment.

We named our plan for a fully integrated system - which I'd still like to push with the VA someday - the "Geisford Delivery Systems," a combination of our surnames and felt like we had put together a very logical and effective solution for the healthcare crisis our nation was facing. We, or should I say I, had to type the whole thing out on an electric typewriter with no autocorrect. We also had to buy the ink and paper from the Bureau of Prisons, just to make it all happen.

If one day we get to trial it successfully, then it could be scaled up to become the new standard healthcare model for the entire country. That's still my dream, and devising that plan gave me a purpose while I was in prison. In fact, I would even go so far as to say it could be the reason I was destined to go to prison: to meet Dr. Stradford and spend nine months together as a de facto two-man prison think tank, working our asses off to put this thing together. I was driven to see the project through because it has helped me see some purpose in all this mess, to make something good out of the bad.

I was working particularly hard because I wanted to make sure we completed it before it was time for me to leave Dr. Stradford behind in prison. When I was released a year into my 15-month sentence, he still had another year to go.

The year I spent in prison wasn't easy, but I'm thankful I had the support of so many friends and family members, who wrote me letters and came to visit me. Sadly enough, a lot of the prisoners never received any mail, but I was flooded with it.

One of the inmates, Blaze, started calling me, "Geise, Geise, Geise," because that's what he often heard as they shouted out names at mail call. I had visitors almost every weekend and knew many people were missing me on the outside and that I had a life I could go back to. Many, if not most, of the other prisoners did not.

Also, my parents looked after my children when they weren't with my ex-wife, so that love, safety, and continuity helped my boys get through that tough year. They stepped in, like two soldiers, and took over the allotted time I would have spent with the boys and had them over at their house instead. They made sure nothing changed for them in that respect. They went to every school function, providing that loving support, just like they'd done for my brothers and me when we were growing up.

And, on weekends, when they could make the trip, my parents brought my boys to Canaan to see me—talk about tugging at your heartstrings. Seeing the boys with my parents was phenomenal, but when they left I had to fight off the incredible depression by getting straight back to work. Saying goodbye to them was always enormously difficult.

My girlfriend filled in as many of the other weekends as she could, driving five-and-a-half hours and checking into a hotel the night before. This way she could enter the prison as soon as visitation started, and we could spend a good part of the day together.

I'm eternally thankful to everyone who reached out to me during that time.

A year is a long time in a child's life, so my absence must have seemed like three years rather than twelve months. That's a time we can never get back. Kids are very resilient, but it's hard to know what deeper effect that year had on them. Only time will tell.

So many of the inmates were young kids themselves, barely out of their teens, often doing long stretches for minor offenses. A good share of those involved marijuana, and I heard so many crazy stories about how the actual dealers "cut deals," and these guys took the fall. I felt so sorry for them, and I still do. I know more than one of them was the product of an unfair system.

Ultimately, although my time in prison was incredibly difficult, it's very humbling to have so many loyal and loving people in my life, and I can't thank them enough for standing by me.

CHAPTER TWENTY-FIVE

FREEDOM

"May we think of freedom not as the right to do as we please, but as the opportunity to do what is right."

- Peter Marshall

A month before the end of my sentence, just when the end was in sight, something happened that threatened to jeopardize my release.

I failed a drug test.

I'd never smoked cigarettes or weed. I'd never done any drugs, and I certainly had never done any of those things while in prison.

It was just the end of a routine day. I'd been dropped off at the camp after work when I was called by one of the guards to perform a random drug test by peeing into a cup. After I had finished, I could see the guard frowning at me. "What's up?" I asked.

"You just failed your piss test. According to this, you're high on amphetamines and barbiturates."

I knew what failing that test meant, and it was not good. G Ward, the bus driver, had failed his piss test earlier in the day and was now sitting in solitary confinement in the maximum security prison.

"What?" I stammered. "With the greatest respect, do I look like I'm drugged up? Do I look like I'm even close to high at the moment? Besides that, I can honestly tell you I have never touched drugs in my entire life, *ever*."

The guard continued to stare accusingly at me.

"I've never even smoked pot." I protested. "My blood, and urine, have to be so goddam clean right now, and how on God's earth would I even get drugs in here anyway? You really think I would risk taking drugs 30 days before my release? There's no way there's anything in my urine. You guys must have bad cups. You guys need to pour my urine into another cup because your cups are malfunctioning, and for this test to be valid, you're going to have to do it before it all cools off."

The guard sighed and dropped his shoulders. "Okay, okay," he said.

Fortunately for me, the guard had enough presence of mind to listen and take the appropriate action. If it had been one of the tougher, less responsive guards on duty that day, I'd have been sent straight to the Special Housing Unit, which in simple terms means solitary confinement in a tiny cell. I think it helped that I was a doctor and that I'd always been respectful and well-behaved toward all the guards during my stretch, regardless of whether they were idiots or bullies. I reasoned that, if I could take orders and keep my head down in the Army, then I could do the same in prison. It was just the smart thing to do.

The guard rang through to his superior to get permission to retest me, and, luckily for me, the answer was yes. So, the guard poured my urine into another cup, and it registered negative for drugs. Thankfully, I escaped spending my last 30 days in solitary and having another month added to my sentence.

G Ward was released from solitary the following day and has no idea why he was allowed to return to the camp, but I was watching his back, and petitioned hard for his release too.

On my final day, I woke early and calmly gathered my belongings together. Anything I had of value I gave to White Mike, who still had another year or so to go. I met up with Dr. Stradford so that we could talk about a more favorable future just one more time. Then I quietly walked away from Camp Canaan with very little fanfare, saying my goodbyes to those I truly respected and ended the morning leaving the same buildings I had entered on my way in.

Larina had driven up the night before and checked into the Waymark Inn. She knew I wouldn't want to spend even an extra minute at Canaan so made sure to arrive early at the prison to pick me up. I was officially released from prison on September 15, 2011.

Even though I had my home in Newfane, each day I was required to report to a halfway house 38 miles away in Buffalo until I could show I was gainfully employed (and release day was no exception).

This daily drive to Buffalo continued for about a month until I got all the official paperwork together to show I was stepping right back into dentistry. My license to practice had not been revoked, and my patients were all waiting for me. Boy, I was more than ready to resume my old life—I couldn't wait. I was so excited. While I'd been in prison, my associate, Dr. Bates, and my entire staff had been working really hard, valiantly trying to cover some of my patients as well as his own—so I owed them all big time. They had indeed kept everything afloat.

On my first day back at the office, my entire staff surrounded me, welcoming me back. In my absence, they'd worked like clockwork, and I could see they'd remained a tight team. I was also fortunate the vast majority of my patients waited for me. I felt very blessed, and I really started to believe I would be able to just pick up with my life again, carry on where I left off, rebuild the trust of my community, and hit the ground running.

I had full days booked well ahead in my schedule, and I was relishing the prospect of getting back to normal. Things appeared to be working out just like my lawyers had assured me. When I had plea-bargained 18 months earlier, it was with the implicit understanding I wanted to keep my license to practice dentistry, and they assured me I should be able to. They did say there would be some questions from the NY State Education Board, but those issues could be handled if they came up. I don't know why I was so confident about this; after all, they'd been wrong about nearly everything else.

Sure enough, by November, I'd started to let my guard down and believed my career was clicking back into place, just as the New York State Education Department contacted me to warn me there might be an issue with my licensure. However, they allowed me to carry on practicing for the time being because I had recently filed not only my appeal but also a civil lawsuit against just about everyone involved in my case—the judge, the district attorney, the three assistant DAs on my case, and, most important of all, my own defense team, Mr. Daniels and Mr. Muscato.

To keep my license, I knew I was going to have to overturn my conviction, and the biggest challenge to achieving that was finding a lawyer to help me navigate the complex process of suing everybody. The legal community professes to hold in high regard the principle that everybody deserves representation, but they all close ranks when you go after one of their own. Indeed, I had to do a lot of the heavy lifting myself. Even when I went to Buffalo to file the legal papers—six copies of everything—I was still met with a lack of cooperation from the legal community that bordered on open hostility.

A few days after I filed, a response was fired right back at me regarding the immunity of the judge, the district attorney, and the assistant DAs. They were immune from prosecution, so that was a dead end. But it wasn't a waste of time because I wanted those guys to read my paperwork and understand I knew how the government had abused the clock and then cobbled all the paperwork together in one document—*seven continuance orders in one day.* I wanted them to know I had uncovered their little fraud, and that was just one of many.

I still had the gratification of suing my defense team for legal malpractice in federal court. That too was quickly dismissed because it wasn't filed in the correct jurisdiction, so I pursued them through the state court. I still didn't have a malpractice lawyer, although it wasn't for lack of throwing money at the problem.

I hired one guy for $10,000 to help me sue Mr. Daniels and Mr. Muscato, but he did virtually nothing other than string me along for a bit until he told me we couldn't file anything—and we never did file. I would have loved to have nailed them for their incompetence, but I shall have to accept the lesser pleasure of letting them know, that I knew, what they did wrong and how ineffective they were at representing me.

Meanwhile, the New York State Education Department was watching my various appeals to overturn my conviction with interest. They allowed me to practice, pending resolution of everything I had submitted to the courts, so that was holding them off for a while longer. By this time, I'd also hired an appellate lawyer to put in a Supreme Court challenge to set aside my convictions because everything had fallen on deaf ears in the appellate court.

I was pleasantly impressed with the work this new lawyer did with my Supreme Court brief, which cost me about $20,000. It was a wild shot. Only a small fraction of the cases that are presented to the Supreme Court are actually heard, but I wanted to have proof I had fought the good fight as hard as I could. Unfortunately, mine was not heard and I was working even harder now to pay for all this on top of all my usual bills.

For my peace of mind and integrity, I had to pursue it, even though it was a huge drain, both financially and emotionally. My kids were now in high school, and, in a few years, my eldest would be in college, so I'd soon have to find the means to help pay for their college interests.

By the spring of the following year, it had become clear none of the legal avenues I had taken were going to have any impact on my conviction, so that's when the New York State Education Department moved in. They sent me a letter stating that, with any criminal conviction, there is a mandatory three-year revocation of licensure.

I strenuously highlighted the anomalies in my case and tried to explain why I believed I should stay in practice. But they simply weren't prepared to listen. The more I tried to convince New York State I was wrongly convicted, the more they *didn't* want to pursue it.

CHAPTER TWENTY-SIX

LOSING MY LIVELIHOOD

"There is nothing so degrading as the constant anxiety about one's means of livelihood."
- W. Somerset Maugham

Eventually, the New York State Department of Education instructed me I would have to forfeit my license in June 2012. According to NY State Law, that also meant I couldn't own a dental practice. But before they could do that, I had to attend a hearing in Albany, where a small panel of my peers (i.e., practicing dentists) was supposed to make the decision.

The panel turned out to be five nonagenarians, none of whom were dentists, from what I could tell—and three of them were either asleep or close to being. Only one of them spoke to me directly. Such was the pedigree of this esteemed cadre of non-dental experts who stripped me of my license.

On top of all this, I still had to check in regularly with my probation officer, so even looking for work was difficult because I had to run everything past him. I couldn't even travel out of Western New York without his permission. Indeed, I always made sure he knew exactly where I was so there was no doubt, but, in all other respects, I was in deep trouble.

I still had an enormous mortgage to pay back on the major new practice I had built in 2001. I'd already paid the restitution the courts said I owed before sentencing, but I was also spending thousands on appeals and lawsuits. Now I had no choice but to sell my practice to my associate for less than it was worth.

I kept ownership of the property, but I lost my livelihood. I applied for several jobs in dental sales, but I didn't get a single interview. I was more than qualified for each of those positions, but my recent past surely played into their decisions not to respond to me. It's pretty tough getting past a felony conviction, much less two. I even tried to develop an online dental product website with very little success. Fortunately, I did make a little rent from some other units within my office complex, and I already owned a historic building in Lockport, next to the Erie Canal (a building I had purchased in 2004 when my dental practice was doing well and before the government set their sights on me).

Over the next few years, I invested a huge amount of effort into that Lockport property, applying for grants to restore the building with the hopes of attracting paying tenants. I also learned a lot about Lockport history, so much so that I became something of an expert—the go-to local amateur historian.

I nearly had to sell that property just to make ends meet, but somehow I managed to keep hold of it. There were plenty of people sniffing around, hoping I had to sell, so they could swoop in and pick up a bargain. With the help of my friend, Dr. Todd Retell, I was able to sign a couple of tenants just in time.

Naturally, I attracted media criticism as soon as the

new tenant applied for one specific grant—asking for handouts for a building I owned—when I'd been convicted of fraud. My tenant had applied for the grant to do capital improvements to her lease space, but that wasn't a big enough story, so the TV reporter made sure to mention my name. "Should a confirmed tax cheat be allowed to apply for tax benefits?"

If you haven't already, you should read, *The Scarlett Letter* by Nathanial Hawthorne. Then you'll know exactly the damage this conviction did to me. In the modern world, a simple search on Google now painted a picture of me that was completely to my disadvantage as I tried to provide health care and rebuild my career. I had no choice but to search for a plan B.

The history of Lockport is fascinating. It dates from the time the Erie Canal was built up to the early 1900s, with the whole Tesla–Edison rivalry centering on the town. Events that occurred during that time were instrumental in the battle between AC and DC electric currents. Edison was very interested in Lockport—the building next to mine is informally known as the Edison building because Edison was all about local power sources electrifying local needs. In Lockport, he could actually see the DC powering the town's streetlights.

My building—2 Pine Street—was utilized by Birdsill Holly, a mechanical engineer and inventor of water hydraulics devices. He developed a unique steam-powered system to pump water into Lockport's city mains to supply not only drinking water but also pressurized water for fire hydrants. My building acted as the testing ground for the very first fire hydrant system, which can now be seen everywhere in the world. I've written more than 30 articles about the history of these Lockport buildings, all completed as I tried to occupy my time while I was unable to continue with dentistry.

As hopeless as my career was looking, and having to wait years before I could get back into dentistry, in 2013 I still hit the jackpot. My girlfriend, Larina, had suffered through the worst of times with me, never once failing to drop everything in her life to keep mine going, so I decided to do something I never thought I would ever do again: I proposed marriage.

But before I could do that, I first needed to speak with her father, Alex, a man I had truly come to respect for all he and his family had endured and survived in the Soviet Union. I was still unemployed, and he knew that, but I was doing everything I could to keep my own kids clothed and fed.

Alex was home from work with a bad knee on the day I called. He never took time off work so I knew his knee must be pretty bad. When I arrived at the house, the front door was already open, and Alex was standing behind the glass storm door with a smile on his face and an ice pack in his hand.

"Mr. Shtarker, how are you? You should be sitting on the couch or something with that ice pack on your knee."

"I'm okay. Frida is still at work, so come in and let's just sit down at the kitchen table."

I knew exactly what I wanted to say, but sometimes his second language, English, wasn't perfect, so I just dove in, "Mr. Shtarker, I hope you know how happy I am to have met your family and how much I care for your daughter, and I stopped by to see you today because I wanted to ask your permission to propose to Larina."

As I said those words, Alex's facial expression didn't change at all. I assumed he didn't quite understand what I'd just said, or maybe some of the words were unfamiliar to him, so I tried again. "I love your daughter. We get along so well, and I hope you can see how happy we are when we're together. I would like to ask for your permission to marry her."

Still, the expression on his face didn't change and I was trying to rephrase once more, when a smile began to spread over his face, and before I could say another word, he said, "All of the pain in my knee just went away."

I hugged him and stayed talking with him for a while, letting him know of my plans to propose to Larina on Mother's Day so both Frida and my parents, and my boys, could all be there. Because the boys were all in on it, we had it set up so they would bring out a Mother's Day gift for Larina.

When she opened the box that contained the ring, I knelt before her and asked her to marry me. It was wonderful surprise for all the moms in the room!

CHAPTER TWENTY-SEVEN

NEW BEGINNINGS

"No matter how hard the past is, you can always begin again."

- Buddha

In fall 2015, after three long years, it was time for me to reapply for my dental license, which was no easy task. Naturally, it meant I had to hire another lawyer who knew how to navigate through this highly nauseating (it literally made me ill), bureaucratic process. The last thing I wanted to do was to have to spend what little money I had on yet another lawyer, but, at this point, what did money matter, and what choice did I have?

I did my research and found a guy in Long Island who seemed to meet all my requirements—someone who knew the Byzantine system and how it operated. I needed this to work the first time, as I couldn't afford to be tied up in a tangle of red tape. I needed to know this guy was the real deal, so I made the nine-hour drive to meet him in person because there was no way I was ever going to hire another legal representative without prior face-to-face contact.

I met him, liked him, and hired him. He was a restless, chain-smoking, highly proficient guy who I will just refer to as Rodney. He explained the process and helped me assemble the correct paperwork and submit the relevant documents. Then we had to wait for the licensing board to convene, which astonishingly was only once a year. The first meeting wasn't until July 2016 (four full years after I had lost my license).

On July 22, 2016, we all showed up at the preliminary meeting in New York City on the tenth floor of a skyscraper in downtown Manhattan. My lawyer accompanied me, and I also had to bring along two character witnesses. My wife Larina was there too. We had married in 2013 in my back garden in Newfane, with my boys standing up as my best men. So of course they were at the preliminary meeting to add their support too (they were now aged 19, 17, and 16). It was Thorne's birthday, and I wanted to make sure we were all there to open this new chapter in my life, and theirs.

My lawyer had prepped me about the importance of being humble and taking responsibility for my conviction. The board didn't want to hear about how I'd been wrongly convicted or let down by my lawyers and the entire stinking legal system all the way up to the judge. They needed to see a chastened man, mortified by his past mistakes, who had damned well learned his lesson. The panel needed to see I owned what I had done, grasped where and why I'd gone wrong, and that I could keep appropriate procedures in place to ensure this would never happen again. In other words, I had to grovel before the panel while my wife and boys watched.

My first character witness was a close friend of mine from Newfane, Gina Guido-Redden, who is also married to one of my best friends, Eoin Walsh. She had known me and my entire family since she was old enough to go to school, and now she ran her own company working with businesses to develop data systems to facilitate their food and drug administration compliance. She was highly professional, sharp as a tack, and very outspoken, and she has even had the opportunity to report to Congress. So I knew she'd be a skilled advocate.

The second witness was Dr. Todd Retell, who had known me since the first day of dental school when we became roommates during the long four years of professional training. He could vouch for my professional competence and integrity, and he knew the details of my case and understood completely the way the system could feign justice. He had also seen firsthand the community spirit I had exhibited throughout my career, and he knew how much time and effort I had put into making Newfane and Lockport better for all, both before and after my conviction.

This time the panel consisted of three people, all of whom at least appeared to be breathing and below the age of 60. One was a dentist, the other was a chiropractor, and I don't know what the other person's specialty was.

The meeting began with the panel interviewing my two character witnesses while my lawyer and I sat at an adjacent table. They did a great job answering all of the panel's questions, and I couldn't have asked for anything better. Then another lawyer provided the panel with the prosecutorial perspective, telling them my crimes were devious and serious, that I was a crook and most likely a recidivist. Then as my lawyer started presenting to the panel, they started asking me some questions. The dentist on the panel did most of the talking. She was keen to understand the coding issues around amalgams.

"Dr. Geise, can you please explain the details concerning the coding issues? It's my understanding you were initially indicted for billing for work that you didn't do. I see that this count was dropped, and the prosecution diverted its attention to fraudulent coding with the insurance companies. Is it correct you coded for items that were of higher value than the work you performed?"

"No, ma'am," I replied. "I submitted for amalgams when I actually supplied composites." Then I made sure to add, "and I know I shouldn't have done that. I know I should have coded for exactly what I did."

"So, what you're saying, is that you supplied a composite but you billed for a less expensive amalgam?"

"That's correct, yes."

"And you actually did the work?"

"That's correct. The prosecution proved it by going to people's houses and taking photographs of their teeth."

"So... you actually gave them something for nothing?"

"That's exactly what I did."

"But why would you do that?" she asked.

"Ma'am, I grew up in this town with these people. I know most if not all of them. I know their grandparents, I know their grandchildren, I know where they live and who lived in their house before they did. It's a small town. If they wanted a composite, I gave them one, but I only charged the price of an amalgam."

She stared at me, somewhat unbelievingly.

"When I submitted for a composite, ma'am," I continued, "the insurance companies would change the code to turn it into an amalgam code and then send it back to me, but they only paid for the amalgam."

"Thank you for clarifying that, Dr. Geise. Now I

understand completely." She turned and glared at the prosecutor. "I don't believe this!" Then, turning back to me, she said, "What were the other counts?"

"Well," I answered, "they found there was an issue with my taxes for three years."

"Do you do your own taxes?"

"No, ma'am, it's far too complicated. I hire a CPA to do my taxes every year."

"And did the CPA get into any trouble—were there any issues with the CPA?"

I shrugged my shoulders, "Well, the prosecution went to talk to him once and then never went back."

"I know how these tax things can go," she said. "Thank you, Dr. Geise, for explaining all that to me so clearly."

Incredible. It was so exciting to have somebody understand my point of view so quickly, using common sense. This put some wind in my sails, and I felt validated and very positive when answering all of the remaining questions. But the panel didn't give me a ruling on the spot. I had to wait about a month to receive a verdict.

My lawyer called me at home. "Congratulations, Dr. Geise, you've made it past the first hurdle."

The panel had unanimously found in my favor, so now I could pass on to the next stage of the process. It was an immense relief, but I couldn't rest on my laurels. I immediately consulted with my lawyer, and we completed all the paperwork and applied for the next stage, showing our favorable judgment from the first panel. After submitting all the paperwork, however, I again had to wait until the next meeting of the board—which was a full six months later.

This time, in January 2017, I drove to Albany with my

wife and met up with my lawyer, Rodney, for the second review. It was a five-hour drive, so we had made the journey the night before and stayed in a hotel. That evening, I spent three hours prepping with Rodney so we could be ready for the panel the following day.

Rodney is a high-intensity guy—smoking a pack of cigarettes a day—and comes across as somewhat disheveled and disorganized. But he has a razor-sharp mind and is highly competent, although some of his methods might appear unconventional.

For example, he told me to watch the scenes in the movie *The Shawshank Redemption*, in which Morgan Freeman's character, Red, keeps getting rejected by the parole board. He said to watch it over and over and over again. Unlike Red, he wanted me to demonstrate my regret, to convince them that, if I could go back and do things differently, I would.

In other words, I had to convey how sorry I was for what I'd done, and that there was absolutely no possibility of anything remotely similar happening again. I had to show I was a changed man, and, again, not an innocent man wrongly accused, misunderstood or let down by a flawed system.

Although, on reflection, that was a bizarre choice of movie, because—spoiler alert—Red's strategy of being penitent, tractable, and polite to the parole board failed time after time. He finally gained his freedom by speaking—somewhat antagonistically, with quiet world-weary defiance—from the heart.

The next day, brimming with genuine remorse and penitence, I faced the second panel. This time, there were three panel members—one guy, who was a chiropractor, and two women, one of whom was a psychologist and the other some kind of intellectual.

Rodney had no forewarning of who was on the panel, but he told me he hoped there would be some women because he thought my physical appearance (tall, reasonably handsome) would hold some sway. I found that hard to believe, but he knew his job, and we were, after all, just a bunch of fallible human beings.

After I had answered several questions from the panel, Rodney must have felt I wasn't nailing all of the key elements we had discussed at the hotel because he suddenly hijacked the proceedings to make a little speech. I'm sure he thought he was rendering an Academy Award-winning monologue when he looked at the psychologist and said, "Look, I'm sure you probably have more degrees than a thermometer, but taxes are a very complicated and tricky thing, you know. It's very easy to keep some cash here and there . . ."

He rambled on for a couple of minutes, and the more he spoke, the more uncomfortable I became. With a knot in my stomach and sweat prickling the back of my neck, I worried he was badly misreading the room. Oh my God, I thought to myself, he might well be ruining my chances here. This guy has watched way too many movies.

When Rodney finally stopped talking, we all shared a brief tumbleweed moment of bemused silence. The panel members remained fairly inscrutable, but I felt I knew enough about human behavior to guess they weren't about to stand on their chairs and break into spontaneous applause.

After a beat, the panel resumed questioning me, and I dutifully demonstrated my abject remorse. I did everything I could—I even told them the story of the day I was leaving for Scranton and had to wave goodbye to my son on the football field, to demonstrate how sorry I was. I didn't need to fake it. There was no way I wanted to go through any of this experience again, so I let my guard down and spoke honestly, simply, and without hyperbole (like Red).

"If I could just get my license back," I begged the panel, "I want to get back to my community. They need me down there. They're asking for me now. I just need to get back home, so I can continue to be there for them." I was in the moment, and it seemed to grip the entire panel.

As we were walking downstairs after the meeting, from the stiffness of his back, I could tell Rodney was furious with me. I must have failed to use some of the key phrases he'd taught me. Whatever it was, he looked ready to burst as we departed the building. When we reached the parking lot, he asked if my wife could go to the car while we walked in the opposite direction so we could talk in private.

Rodney's hands were shaking as he lit up a cigarette. Then he laid into me. "You just fucking screwed the pooch. What were you thinking? You totally missed—why the hell did we spend three hours last night going over all this? I spent all this time with you. I just cannot believe you didn't hit the points. It was simple. I hate fucking losing. You're a smart guy, right? You should be able to remember three friggin things!"

"Look," I said, "I think it was more important that I told the goddam truth. That's what matters. That's what they want to hear. It's obvious I was telling the truth, and there was no way I would ever do anything like that again."

"You're wrong. You ruined everything. You're screwed, and I hate goddamn losing."

He stormed off to his car and screeched away while I walked slowly back to my wife, feeling very shaken, sick, and miserable.

Did I really misjudge things so badly?

Was this the end of my career?

Had the last four-and-a-half years been a complete waste of time?

Is the system so blind as not to see the truth of what really happened to me?

I didn't have any of the answers.

CHAPTER TWENTY-EIGHT

LICENSED TO FILL

"The best way out is always through."

- Robert Frost

We drove the next five hours in silence. All I could do was concentrate on the road and the humming that was in my ears. Stewing silently, I was furious with myself for destroying my chances of returning to dentistry, but, at the same time, I felt confused that somehow my instincts had proven so misplaced.

Larina tried to lighten the mood. "You know, we've got to just hope for the best. What else can we do?"

But there was nothing she could say to bring me back from the depths of my despair. All I could think was that I was never going to get my career back—because, once you get knocked out of the system, you have to start all over again after waiting another three years. I sat through that miserable journey planning alternative careers because I thought I'd sure as hell stunk up my chances of being a dentist any time soon.

I had the real estate business, but I had to figure out a way to earn a better than decent living because of my overhead. I had three boys heading to college, or so I hoped. I pondered whether I should put more energy into the nonprofit in Lockport, and that maybe I could do something financially rewarding by providing tours of the area. I was just going to have to make the best of things, put my head down, and grind away until I could reapply in three years.

Surprisingly, one month later, I received an email from Rodney. He congratulated me on receiving a unanimous decision from that recent panel, allowing me to move on to the next step of regaining my license. He made no apology for having ripped me a new one after the hearing. But that good news was the best possible outcome for my bruised ego and my professional future.

The two panels I had completed were the most exacting and the most difficult hurdles. According to Rodney, the rest was almost a rubber-stamping process. As long as those people on those boards were in favor of my reinstatement, and unless something came in from left field, I would be back in business.

After reading the email, I immediately called Rodney and blurted out my thanks for his letter. "How long before I can move forward?" I asked. "We've got six out of six here, so we're in good shape. Do you think we can get all this sorted by the end of March?"

"Oh, no," said Rodney, exhaling loudly. "The panel won't meet again until December."

"But that's nine months away!"

"What they'll do is review the decision of those two panels and then decide if you can move forward," he said.

"But, what's there to decide? It's taken two years for me to face two panels, and now I've got to wait almost another whole year? This is crazy."

Before all was said and done, I would have to tread water for another thirteen months. In the meantime, I focused on my real estate, kept developing the nonprofit, and got through another Christmas as a nondentist. In February 2018, I received a letter from the third panel, which had met up in New York and approved my reinstatement, once I "completed 60 hours of continuing education."

Fortunately, I'd already been continuing my education. I'd been doing online CE for several years to ensure I was staying on top of the current best practices in dentistry. I mean, what else was I going to do? It's not as if I didn't have hours of spare time. I already had nearly 60 hours under my belt.

I contacted the panel to let them know I was close to fulfilling my CE obligations. They instructed me to send my CE credits to prove I had met the requirements and it wasn't long before I received a letter back explaining they could only count the credits from the current year. Since it was only February, they were only accepting CE from the current year, which wiped out all but 10 hours of those credits. Now I had to find another 50 credit hours before I could practice again.

From February to May 2018, I attended the requisite courses in person, filling them up with any subject I could find—sleep apnea, Botox, anything that fit the bill. When I had completed all of them and submitted proof of all the additional credits, only then did they mail me back my license to practice dentistry.

I remember so clearly the day my license arrived— simply an envelope in the post, quietly, anonymously, and without any fanfare. It had been placed at my front door on the doormat. Hard to believe that this tiny piece of paper gave me back my livelihood and a significant chunk of my self-respect.

As a practical matter, it allowed me to reenter society, engage fully with my local community again, and feel like a useful human being. Not only could I earn a proper living, but I could also hold my head a little higher, even though no one else in town had any idea as to the sacrifices it took to get my life back.

Yet, for some reason, I felt curiously hollow. It's not as if I wanted to jump around the room and wave my license in the air. After 10 years of fighting *The Man*, I was hit by this incomprehensible wave of utter exhaustion.

I'd read that's how trauma works. But reading a medical journal is one thing—feeling it in the flesh, quite another. Recently, I'd read an article somewhere in which paramedics described how common it is for severely injured people to undergo a full mind and body crash the moment they're safely inside an ambulance.

As victims, they'd been able to cling to life until help arrived, but then their bodies shut down the moment they felt they were in safe hands. One of the paramedics had said she never uses phrases like "you're safe" or "leave it to us," because it sends the wrong signal; it tells the victim to stop fighting, when, in reality, the victim needs to stay present and conscious and continue to use all their willpower to stay alive.

My youngest son Thorne's 17th birthday was approaching again in July. I calculated he had been six years old when this nightmare started; Myles was eight, Stone only 10. No kidding. I'd been battling the system at a time that they needed me most, and I'd had to deal with so much uncertainty and stress through those years that it must have bled through to them.

I felt I missed out on so much with my boys simply because I'd been preoccupied with so many other unnecessary and unjustified things. So, at that moment in time, regaining my license didn't feel like a total victory—or even a victory at all. It had taken so long to get to this point that the shine had worn off and left me numb.

I made a cup of coffee and stared at the letter and the jagged end of the envelope where I'd hastily ripped it open. A semiotics professor could have written an entire book on what that letter represented, not just to me in the practical here and now but equally in a wider context. I'd fought for a decade to reach this point in my life, but I felt rung out, numb, and drained.

I remember studying the Ancient Greek philosophers in high school, which is why I probably felt so compelled to go to Greece while I was overseas. It was tough going at the time, but one of the phrases that has, for some reason, stuck with me concerns suffering.

Staring at that letter, I realized that, for years, I'd been feeling empty and disconnected from the world. Aristotle, the Greek philosopher, living between 384–322 BC, said, "Suffering becomes beautiful when anyone bears great calamities with cheerfulness, not through insensibility but through greatness of mind."

So, back from the wintry exile I came, and now all I had to do was find a job. My first thought was to go back to my former associate, Dr. Bates, who now owned my old practice in downtown Newfane and had been practicing there on his own for the last six years under the new name of "Newfane Dental."

At first, my desires were very humble. All I wanted to do was go back to work as an associate and at least do some procedures—dermal filler, sleep apnea, anything I knew he didn't do—so I wouldn't be taking work from him. He was also my tenant, so I had a strong incentive, morally and financially, to protect his current level of income.

With these thoughts in mind, I ultimately decided to set up in one of my buildings across the parking lot from Dr. Bates. While I was fitting out that new office, I was applying for dental positions anywhere and everywhere in Western New York so I could pick up some extra part-time hours to supplement my income. I received one nibble, from a two-dentist operation in Buffalo called the Smile Center.

When I met the owner of the Smile Center, Dr. Gordon Kent, I had to be totally upfront about my past and my criminal conviction. Fully expecting him to chase me out the door with a bat, I was pleasantly surprised when he listened attentively, albeit with an inscrutable expression on his face.

When I had finished telling him my story, Gordon smiled and told me his father was a dentist and that, coincidentally, had gone through something similar to me. So, rather than find a hostile detractor, I'd found the opposite: a dentist with strong sympathy for what I'd been through.

"I know things happen," Gordon said. "I know how these things work. And I know you've owned and run your own practice, but I'd like to start you off part-time, a couple of days a week if you can do that. Just to test the waters, if you know what I mean."

242

"I'd love to!" I practically yelled. It was such a great feeling, not only to be employed by a fellow dentist but to actually be *employable*. Certainly owing to his father's similar experience, Dr. Kent was the only person who felt comfortable enough with me to take that chance.

Before I knew it, on June 1, 2018, I was seeing patients at the Smile Center in Buffalo, with the consequent effect that I backed off on getting my Newfane office sorted out. I'd waited six years for this, but, during those six years, I hadn't so much as looked at a dental tool, let alone used one.

I'm not going to lie: those first few patient consultations were terrifying, as I refamiliarized myself with procedures I previously had been able to do with my eyes shut. Not only did I have to remember how to do all the routine stuff, but dentistry had also progressed with new takes on old procedures and new procedures I'd never seen before.

Though taking it slow at first, within a few weeks, I was on fire and couldn't wait to get to work. Like a kid, I was so excited to be doing dentistry again. Quickly I got back on top of my game and produced so much revenue for the practice it shocked everyone. Gordon had hit a gold mine.

But that's not to say all was hunky-dory. To this day, we still have issues with insurance companies. They know about my felony past, and I'm still grappling with New York State because they put me on a Medicare and Medicaid exclusion list based solely on my conviction, and I have had to hire yet another lawyer to remove me from that list.

I can treat some patients in these insurance plans, but,

if I do, the carriers must send the check directly to the patient and make it out in THEIR name. Most of the time, that means the office doesn't get paid because the patient assumes the check is an insurance rebate, and why wouldn't they? So naturally they keep the money with their name on it, not realizing they're supposed to use it to pay us.

The logistics are a nightmare, and other insurance companies refuse to let me work for them simply because of that exclusion list, so it has wider repercussions. It's an ongoing battle. I am still in the process of being reinstated by many of these insurance plans. Furthermore, in some areas of public life, my conviction has been nothing less than a life sentence, because I must constantly fight the system to win back the same freedoms I once had. To have your integrity questioned at every turn is not something I would wish on anyone. And as the saying goes, there's always someone out there dreaming of having the same freedoms that most of us simply take for granted. At this point in my life, I was that someone.

The point is that a conviction robs you of those freedoms. I agree that, if you try to take advantage of the system, taking advantage of others for your own benefit, you should be punished. But once that person has been punished, and they have paid their price back to society, they should be allowed to carry on just like all law-abiding citizens.

But this is not the reality—not by a long shot.

CHAPTER TWENTY-NINE

PRACTICE NOT PERFECT

"Let your hopes, not your hurts, shape your future."
- Robert H. Schuller

My ultimate faith in the goodness of humanity compelled me not to give up, even when I was sent to prison. Taking advantage of our time together, Dr. Stradford and I dug into the problems that plague our current American healthcare system. As a result, the idea for the Geisford Delivery System (GDS) was born with the hope of revolutionizing healthcare delivery in America and saving millions of lives.

I have always felt dentistry should have a larger role in our overall healthcare system. Therefore, I approached a woman by the name of Fern Beaver at the VA hospital in Buffalo with the prospect of applying the GDS to our vets. There's no group more deserving of timely and effective health care than those who have protected our freedoms.

Surprisingly, Fern told me I was just the guy she'd been looking and waiting for. She said she'd been trying to set up something similar and could totally see how the GDS could eventually spread from Buffalo to the whole country. Unfortunately, Fern had some health issues of her own and sadly passed away before we could develop the GDS any further.

At present, there's zero collaboration between dentistry and other clinical physicians—which, in my opinion, is a grievous systemic error. In the GDS model, when soldiers come through the VA, they would receive both a medical and dental exam because they are interrelated.

If a cardiologist fixes your heart issue, and you also have periodontal disease, sending bacteria to the valves of your heart, it won't be long before the same procedure will have to be done all over again.

In other words, you can't do one without careful consideration of the other. But, at present, there's nothing to coordinate between the two needs and treatments. Sharing patient information in this way will cut costs, save time, and provide better health care—a win, win, win for all concerned.

And, to reinforce my argument, when I was completing my sleep apnea course for my CE credits, I met two resident dentists from Buffalo VA, and asked them lots of questions, one of which was, "When was the last time you guys talked to a physician to cross-reference care?"

They both replied they had no relationship with the physicians at all, which is insane. They weren't in a position to be able to do so. Yet as a dentist, I'm often required to clear a dental procedure first with a physician. In the meantime, if there's a long delay in getting a response from the cardiologist, the patient is forced to wait on scheduling with us. It's enormously inefficient and ineffective. I want to change all that.

One of the major complaints I hear from new patients

walking into our dental office is they have to fill out a new medical history every time they see a new doctor. Not only do many people not know their medical histories, but even those who do often omit many important details and provide incorrect information. No person can remember it all, especially when incapacitated or diminished.

If I can persuade the VA to adopt the GDS model, the cost of effective medical and dental care will drop radically. In 2021, health care in the United States costs about $12,000 annually per American. The GDS model could theoretically cut that in half over time, relieving much of the current stress on the American healthcare system.

Although Dr. Stradford is practicing as a dentist, he's also working with technical experts to start up a telemedicine platform that integrates dentistry and patient dental records with other medical disciplines. Our whole program was always about enabling routine collaboration between specialties daily, and both of us continue to work toward that end.

I have also joined a national organization called the American Academy of Oral Systemic Health, which is a national network of healthcare professionals and advocates who are dedicated to expanding awareness of the relationship between oral health and whole body health. I'm convinced they're on the right track to making a system-wide change by bringing more professionals together. Through more interaction, we can learn from each other.

Dr. Stradford's telemedicine platform, DentRx.net, already allows patients to remotely contact their dentist and talk about a dental problem without having to make an in-person visit, which might otherwise be difficult or impractical. If a patient's physician is also on the platform, the savings in terms of time and costs can be significant.

Ordinarily, if patients come into the office, I take a look at their teeth, and, if treatment is called for, I book a longer appointment on another day to perform the treatment. That's two appointments right there, one of which could be avoided by remote diagnosis. The insurance companies also love it because it costs much less to offer a teleconsultation than to see a patient in the office. So, again, everybody wins.

This added convenience also means patients are far more likely to approach dentists or doctors with their preexisting problems. They get timely treatment, and the outcome is improved in terms of preventative medicine, especially for those people who are more reluctant to visit the clinic in the first place. It especially improves accessibility for people who find it difficult to travel due to work restrictions, disability, cost of travel, COVID-19, you name it.

One significant challenge will be making this technology available to people with poor IT skills or people who have limited access to a computer, mobile phone, or tablet. That will need looking at, but, for the majority of the population, it's a big win right out of the box. And we're not talking hypothetically: the patient portal is up and running right now. Check it out for yourself at DentRx.net.

Faith is something you can't touch, see, or hold in your hand. It's something you just have to have. It's something that keeps you going, keeps you believing, keeps you strong, and enables you to keep chasing those dreams.

I'm lucky to have emerged from my harrowing journey with my faith and my ideals intact. Nothing will stop me from pursuing those dreams and turning them into reality—while remaining forever grateful for the strength, love, and support of my wonderful family and friends.

I pray almost every day, and, in general, I don't ask for much. I pray that my family and friends continue to be happy and healthy, but I do ask for my own wisdom so I can make a difference while I'm still here.

As Carl Schurz, former American statesman and passionate supporter of liberal democracy, once famously said, "Ideals are like stars; you will not succeed in touching them with your hands. But like the sailor at sea, you choose them as your guides, and following them you will reach your destiny."

EPILOGUE

"There are five important things for living a successful and fulfilling life: never stop dreaming, never stop believing, never give up, never stop trying, and never stop learning."

- Roy Bennett

Writing this book has been extremely difficult for me. Primarily, I did it for my family and my friends, so they would learn and know the truth about the horrific ordeal I endured. But I also did it out of a sense of outrage and protest, and to be a good citizen in a democracy.

I have long since forgiven those who have trespassed against me, but I still feel the need to accurately tell my side of the story. It's been painful - beyond description - to relive in excruciating detail the ordeal of my wrongful indictment, wrongful incarceration, and, most importantly, my wrongful guilty plea.

Yet, notwithstanding my ordeal, I'm now able to treat those patients who still trust me. Regardless of everything that was taken from me, I'm still able to make a living and support my family. And I'm still able to hold my head high because I know the truth about what really happened.

True, I should never have placed all my trust in my lawyers and should never have been put in a position to have to plead guilty. But I did and was, and I realize I must take full responsibility for that decision.

So why write a book at all, you may ask? Maybe George Orwell said it best: "If liberty means anything at all, it means the right to tell people what they do not want to hear."

I also reference Roy Leslie Bennett—Google him if you don't know his full story. Although he was imprisoned in Zimbabwe, subject to conditions far worse than my own, his struggle is not unlike mine. Because he too was the victim of government corruption.

When you're going through hell, there's only one way through it, and that is to keep on truckin' and pray the light you see at the end of the tunnel is not another truck. For 15 years now, my horrific experience with the American judicial system has haunted me, dominating and disrupting my life.

By writing this book, I had hoped to revisit everything honestly, with 20–20 hindsight, and then put it behind me forever. To some degree, that has worked. But let me tell you something: You can't ever fully purge your past when it has haunted you for so long.

I recall the days when I first started writing. Every time I put pen to paper, slowly building momentum, I had to stop. Reliving the experience was more than I could bear. I would have to go for a run or take a walk through the park. Or I would have to tell myself to stop it and go do something else.

But then I would recall what Coach Beilein taught us back in high school, so many decades ago. "Son, sometimes you have to take one on the chin for the team, stand back up, and then keep working hard until you get the job done."

As a practicing dentist, I didn't know anything about the legal system when I first got a visit from the FBI. I had never dealt with federal investigators or federal prosecutors before, and I had no idea how to get them to listen to my side of the story—a side that was much closer to the truth than what they had been told.

At the very beginning, when most defendants would have pled the fifth and refused to talk, I was more than happy to answer any questions they had. I felt I had nothing to hide, so I wanted to be very forthcoming with my government, especially when they clearly expressed that I was not a target of their investigation. And when they decided to focus on me, I was never officially arrested and have never been read my Miranda rights.

Back then, I didn't know the reality of criminal investigations. I thought they were about truth, justice, and preserving the American way. But that was very naïve of me. I would learn, painfully, that many criminal prosecutions are about something else entirely. They are about deterrence and money and agenda and political careers.

Oftentimes right or wrong doesn't even enter into the picture. It certainly didn't play a role in my case.

If you're ever accused criminally of anything, even when you know that you aren't involved, don't say anything to anyone, especially the FBI, without a great criminal defense lawyer at your side. Contrary to what I once believed, the agent involved may not be an upstanding human being and, most likely, will not be your friend.

From all the sports teams I have been involved in, I

also know there can be a few bad players on every team. Even some of the most respected agencies in the world have weaknesses—for they're run by human beings, some of whom may have weak tendencies and all of whom, myself included, suffer from some imperfection or another.

If prosecutors need to prosecute, the FBI is there to get them enough information so they can. Therefore, it's crucial if you can't afford a lawyer to be by your side, you remain silent—because anything you say can and will be used against you in a court of law in the most brutal way possible.

You might be asking yourself, "Well, if defense attorneys can't defend us in federal court, why don't we defend ourselves?"

Put simply, the legal system has been designed to make it almost impossible to competently represent yourself in court. There's nearly zero accountability for prosecutors who abuse the rules and laws set forth by Congress, so when prosecutorial misconduct does occur, it's rarely challenged.

When I was accused, I knew I was innocent, and because I was innocent, I wanted my lawyers to help me prove my innocence. Naively, I thought it was just a matter of getting the facts across to the FBI and the prosecutors. Then my lawyers gave me a reality check.

"Doc," they said, "the government can do just about anything it wants to do."

"You're kidding me," I said.

"No, we're not. They can do just about anything they want to!"

Few of us have ever taken the time to read our

Constitution. But when I was given plenty of time, rather than wasting it, I finally did so, and I wish it had been required reading when I went to high school or even college. If I had understood it better, I would have made wiser decisions when the big bad wolf came huffing and puffing at my door.

Of the 80,000 or so federal criminal cases filed every year, less than 400 end in acquittals. Those are not good odds if you're a defendant. The feds have all the resources of the federal government, total credibility, and the presumption of guilt (despite jury instructions to the contrary) on their side.

Don't think for one moment you're presumed anything but guilty, guilty, guilty, because why would the federal government of these United States ever prosecute an innocent man?

In the end, I went to prison. And there I endured the stigma and judgment of what going to prison and being convicted of a crime fully entails. Now and forever after, I have to deal with the unjustified label of *felon* wherever I go in business. Through it all, however, I continue to give to my community, whether they know it or not.

Even when I felt I couldn't fall any lower, I remained optimistic that something good would come out of all the misery that my family and I had been through, for I realized long ago we all must endure some hardship.

Through this process, I found out who my true friends are, and I was fortunate to have such a strong family support system.

Through this process, I found a truly amazing woman to spend the rest of my life with. She has stood by my side at every turn.

Through this process, my children have weathered the storm with us, graduating from college, with bright futures ahead—one in medicine, one in aerospace engineering, and one in business/real estate.

After years of financial hardship, I'm finally getting back to doing what I love to do: serving others by taking care of their dental needs. It might not seem that exciting to you, but I sure love it.

And toward that end, can you believe it? As of May 2023, I have completed my five-year probationary period with New York State, which means all the restrictions the NYS Education Department has imposed on me, and my licensure, have been lifted.

I still love Newfane and its surrounding communities, but I just don't have the same ability to give to it as I had before.

A decade and a half later, my life and liberty have finally been returned to me.

Hallelujah and God bless America.

~

A final note: No A.I. was involved in the writing of this book. It was written by human beings with 100 percent human content.

APPENDIX A

PLEA AGREEMENT

The defendant, SCOTT D. GEISE, and the United States Attorney for the Western District on New York (hereinafter "the government") hereby enter into a plea agreement with the terms and conditions as set out below.

I. THE PLEA AND POSSIBLE SENTENCE

1. The defendant agrees to plead guilty to Count 3 of the Indictment charging a violation of Title 18, United States Code, Section 1035 (false statements relating to health care matters), for which the maximum possible sentence is a term of imprisonment of 5 years, a fine of $250,000, a mandatory $100 special assessment and a term of supervised release of up to 3 years; and to Count 63 of the indictment charging a violation of Title 26, United States Code, Section 7206 (1) (filing a false tax return), for which the maximum possible sentence is a term of imprisonment of 3 years, a fine of $250,000, a mandatory $100 special assessment and a term of supervised release of up to 1 year. The defendant understands that the penalties set forth in this paragraph are the maximum penalties that can be imposed by the Court at sentencing.

2. *The defendant understands that the Court must require restitution as follows: (1) in the amount of $12,479 (for bleach kits billed as occlusal guards) and $17,058 (for sealants billed as amalgams) to be paid to Delta Dental of Michigan; (2) in the amount of $1,567.85 (for sealants billed as amalgams) to be paid to Delta Dental of New York; (3) in the amount of $702.50 (for bleach kits billed as occlusal guards) and $1,235.10 (for sealants billed as amalgams) to be paid to Aetna; (4) in the amount of $403.20 (for bleach kits billed as occlusal guards) and $20 (for sealants billed as amalgams) to be paid to Health Now (Blue Cross/Blue Shield); (5) in the amount of $2,456.20 (for sealants billed as amalgams) to be paid to Guardian; (6) in the amount of $3,886.60 (for sealants billed as amalgams) to be paid to MetLife; (7) in the amount of $214.40 (for sealants billed as amalgams) to be paid to United Concordia, as part of the sentence pursuant to Sentencing Guidelines 5E1.1 and Title 18, United States Code, Section 3663A. The defendant specifically reserves his right to challenge the amount of restitution owed to the above insurance companies for billing sealants as amalgams.*

[This is very important because my lawyers never did challenge the amount of restitution owed before sentencing. Either way, I made sure I paid off all the restitution so the judge would be more lenient on me.]

The defendant further agrees to pay restitution to the Internal Revenue Service in the amount of $58,254.97 (to satisfy defendant's corporate tax liability for Newfane Family dentistry (NFD) for the fiscal years 2003, 2004, and 2005) and in the amount of $29,527.00 (to satisfy defendant's personal income tax liability for the tax years

2002, 2003, 2004, and 2005) as part of the sentence pursuant to Title 18, United States Code, Section 3663 (a) (3). The defendant understands that the payment of restitution pursuant to this plea agreement will not relieve him of any responsibility for any taxes, penalties, and interest that may be owing to the IRS in relation to any civil tax proceedings pending or to be pending against the defendant or any entity in which the defendant has had an interest during any tax year at issue.

3. The defendant understands that, if it is determined that the defendant has violated any of the terms or conditions of supervised release, the defendant may be required to serve in prison all or part of the term of supervised release, up to 2 years, without credit for time previously served on supervised release. As a consequence, in the event the defendant is sentenced to the maximum term of incarceration, a prison term imposed for a violation of supervised release may result in the defendant serving a sentence of imprisonment longer than the statutory maximum set forth in paragraph 1 of this agreement.

II. ELEMENTS AND FACTUAL BASIS

4. The defendant understands the nature of the offenses set forth in paragraph 1 of this agreement and understands that if this case proceeded to trial, the government would be required to prove beyond a reasonable doubt the following elements of the crimes:

a. With respect to Count 3 of the Indictment:

(1) That on or about August 7, 2002, the defendant made, or caused to be made, a material statement or representation, or made or used a material writing or

document, which statement or document involved a health care benefit program;

(2) That the statement, representation, document or writing, was false, fictitious, or fraudulent;

(3) That the false, fictitious, or fraudulent statement or writing was made or created knowingly and willfully; and

(4) That the statement, representation or writing was made in a matter involving the delivery of, or payment for, health care benefits, items or services.

b . With respect to Count 63 of the Indictment:

(1) That the defendant made or caused to be made, and signed income tax returns for the year 2003 that were false to a material matter;

(2) The return contained a written declaration that it was made under the penalty of perjury;

(3) The defendant did not believe the return to be true and correct as to the material matter charged in the Indictment; and

(4) The defendant made, or caused to be made, and signed the return willfully.

5. The defendant and the government agree to the following facts, which form the basis for the entry of the plea of guilty including relevant conduct:

COUNT 3 – FALSE STATEMENTS RELATING TO HEALTH CARE MATTERS

a. During the time period relevant to this Indictment and to this plea agreement, General Motors and/or Delphi, which used to be part of General Motors, had a self-insured insurance plan, which was administered by Delta Dental of Michigan ("Delta Dental"). In addition, Aetna and Blue Cross and Blue Shield of Western New

York ("BC/BS") are companies which sell dental care insurance programs to their subscribers. These programs (hereinafter referenced as "private insurance plans") pay for certain dental services and procedures rendered to the subscribers. As such, these programs are health care benefit programs as defined in Title 18, United States Code, Section 24(b).

b. These private insurance plans also pay for occlusal guards provided to subscribers, when there is a documented medical need for the occlusal guard. An occlusal guard is provided to persons who suffer from clenching and/or grinding of their teeth.

[Patients don't have to be suffering from anything to warrant having a guard made for them. Most people who grind have no idea they're doing it, so, in many cases, the guard is made simply to protect the work that has been done.]

c. Dental providers enter contracts with private insurance plans in which they agree to treat patients in return for certain payments set forth in the contract. The providers agree to various terms and conditions for reimbursement, including, in some cases, the collection of a mandatory co-payment from patients.

d. In order to receive payment for rendering a treatment covered by a private insurance program, a dental provider must submit an American Dental Association ("ADA") dental claim form setting forth the patient's name, the treatment/service provided, date of treatment/service, and a certification by the provider that the treatment/service is in progress or was actually rendered.

[Here, again, is proof the government was turning a

blind eye to my potential involvement in the abandoned Count 1. Here, they pointed out all the requirements needed for a legitimate "bill" to be accepted for payment. They knew I had no responsibility for that original count, but, for some reason, they pushed it through and managed to establish a case against me anyways.]

A claim form can be submitted by mail or it can be electronically submitted to the insurance company.

e. The defendant, SCOTT GEISE, is licensed by New York State as a dentist. GEISE maintains an office named Newfane Family Dentistry (NFD), located at 2727 Main Street, Newfane, New York. GEISE was a preferred provider for Delta Dental of Michigan.

f. During the period from approximately 2002 through 2006, the defendant rendered treatments and provided services to numerous individuals whose treatments and services were covered by private insurance programs. The defendant submitted claim forms to the private insurance programs in order to receive payments for treatments and services rendered to those individuals.

g. During that period, the defendant, SCOTT GEISE, devised and employed a scheme to defraud the private insurance programs, Aetna and BC/BS, and the administrator of a private insurance program, including Delta Dental, which covered his patients by submitting false claim forms to and receiving unearned payments from the insurance companies. The way that the defendant's fraudulent scheme worked is that certain patients asked for a bleach whitening kit, which is a cosmetic item used to bleach a person's teeth, the defendant and/or the defendant's employees would bill the patient's insurance company for an occlusal guard, which is a special mouth guard meant to treat people who grind their teeth at night. The insurance companies covered occlusal guards, because occlusal guards serve a specific medical purpose, but they did not cover bleach whitening kits so by billing the bleach whitening kits as occlusal guards, the defendant was able to receive money from the insurance companies.

h. For example, as charged in Count 3 of the Indictment, on or about August 7, 2002, the patient identified as PAS obtained a bleach whitening kit from the defendant because PAS wanted to whiten PAS's teeth. Defendant GEISE thereafter submitted an ADA dental claim form to Delta Dental seeking payment for providing patient PAS with an occlusal guard: At the time defendant GEISE submitted this claim, the defendant knew that patient PAS had not received an occlusal guard, but rather, had received a bleach whitening kit. Defendant GEISE further knew that the bleach whitening kit provided to patient PAS served no medical purpose, and therefore, was not covered by Delphi's self-insured dental plan, which was administered by Delta Dental.

i. The defendant employed an additional scheme to defraud General Motors and/or Delphi's self-insured dental insurance plan by billing Delta Dental for placing amalgams (silver fillings) in the teeth of several patients, when, in fact, the defendant simply applied sealants on the teeth of the patients. Because the self-insured dental insurance plan did not cover sealants for these patients, but did cover amalgams, the defendant was able to receive money from the insurance plan that the defendant was not entitled to receive.

j. A comparison of defendant GEISE's handwritten

clinical notes and the defendant's billing records reveals conclusively that during the time period under review GEISE submitted false and fraudulent bills to various insurance companies for which he received payment totaling approximately $40,022.85.

[Even though the original Count 1—regarding the Tony Fazzolari "bill"—had been dropped, it magically popped up again in the plea agreement.]

k. For purposes of relevant conduct, defendant GEISE agrees that in or about December 2001, he provided Anthony Fazzolari with a dental bill, in the amount of $6,970, for dental services that defendant GEISE never provided to Anthony Fazzolari. In or about January 2002, Anthony Fazzolari utilized this false dental bill to unlawfully abstract money from Fazzolari's Local 91 Welfare Fund, Personal Account Program . . .

(The document then moves onto:)

COUNT 63 – FILING FALSE INCOME TAX RETURN

1. At all relevant times, NFD accepted United States Currency, checks, credit cards, and insurance payments as forms of payment for services rendered to clients.

m. At all relevant times, Scott D. Geise and NFD utilized Dentrix, a software program designed specifically for use in a dentist's office to keep track of patients, checkups, appointments, billing and patient information.

n. Beginning on or about January 1, 2002, and continuing until approximately December 31, 2005, Scott D. Geise did devise a scheme whereby Scott D. Geise directed his office employees to record cash payments received from patients as credit adjustments in the

Dentrix program. NFD utilized Dentrix to initially record any and all payments it received from patients for services rendered. Subsequently, business receipts including cash were deposited into NFD's Bank of America Account number 9421641325 as a normal business practice. Appropriate entries were then made in NFD's QuickBooks to record the patient fees received as business income.

o. Scott D. Geise admits that all cash receipts recorded as credit adjustments in Dentrix were not deposited into NFD's Bank of America Account number 942164132. Scott D. Geise further admits that the aforementioned cash receipts were not recorded as income in NFD's QuickBooks.

p. Scott D. Geise agrees that NFD reported its yearly business activity to the IRS utilizing a fiscal year ending June 30th. NFD's corporate tax returns (Forms 1120) were prepared at the end of each fiscal year by an accountant. The accountant prepared NFD's Forms 1120 based upon the income recorded in NFD's QuickBooks. Scott D. Geise agrees he was responsible for providing the accountant with true, correct, and complete information in order to prepare Forms 1120 for NFD. Scott D. Geise agrees that he willfully failed to provide the accountant with true, correct, and complete information, concerning the cash income that was not recorded in NFD's QuickBooks which subsequently caused NFD's income to be under-reported.

q. For the fiscal years ending June 30, 2003; June 30, 2004; and June 30, 2005; Scott D. Geise, as owner of Newfane Family Dentistry, P.C. filed with the Internal Revenue Service corporate tax returns, Forms 1120, for

NFD. For each of the aforementioned fiscal years, Scott D. Geise willfully failed to report on these tax returns cash received from patients resulting from the scheme mentioned above. The defendant's willful actions caused the gross profit of NFD to be under-reported and, as a result, falsely reported the amount of tax due and owing to the Internal Revenue Service.

r. Specifically, on or about September 16, 2003, the defendant filed with the IRS a United States Corporate Tax Return, Form 1120 for the fiscal year ending June 30, 2003. Scott D. Geise signed this tax return under the penalties of perjury knowing full well that the tax return was not true and correct as to every material matter.

s. The amount of NFD's corporate tax due and owing to the Internal Revenue Service is listed in the following table:

Items	Fiscal Year Ending 06/30/2003	Fiscal Year Ending 06/30/2004	Fiscal Year Ending 06/30/2005
Taxable Income per Returns	($3,106.00)	$0.00	S11,847.00
Add: Unreported Business Cash Receipts	$75,519.20	$50,371.05	$62,150.22
Subtract: Charitable Contribution Deduction Allowed	($7,241.00)	($5,037.00)	($6,215.00)
Equals: Corrected	$65,172.20	$45,334.05	$67,782.22

Taxable Income			
Corrected Tax Liability	$22,810.27	$15,866.92	$23,723.78
Less: Tax per Return	$0.00	$0.00	($4,146.00)
Additional Tax Due & Owing	$22,810.27	$15,866.92	$19,577.78
Combined Additional Tax Due and Owing	$58, 254. 97		

[The plea agreement also adjusted the offense levels of the two counts to which I would plead guilty.] The result was:

"15. It is the understanding of the government and the defendant that with a total offense level of 14 and criminal history category of I, the defendant's sentencing range would be a term of imprisonment of 15 to 21 months, a fine of $4,000 to $40,000, and a period of supervised release of 2 to 3 years. Notwithstanding this, the defendant understands that at sentencing the defendant is subject to the minimum and maximum penalties set forth in paragraph 1 of this agreement."

IV. STATUTE OF LIMITATIONS

18. In the event the defendant's pleas of guilty are withdrawn, or convictions vacated, either pre- or post-sentence, by way of appeal, motion, post-conviction proceeding, collateral attack or otherwise, the defendant agrees that any charges dismissed pursuant to this agreement shall be automatically reinstated upon motion of the government and further agrees not to assert the statute of limitations as a defense to any other criminal offense involving or related to the filing of false tax returns, making false statements relating to a health care matters, and the unlawful abstraction of money from an employee welfare benefit plan, which is not time barred as of the date of this agreement. This waiver shall be effective for a period of six months following the date upon which the withdrawal of the guilty pleas or vacating of the convictions becomes final.

VI. APPEAL RIGHTS

22. The defendant understands that Title 18, United States Code, Section 3742 affords a defendant a limited right to appeal the sentence imposed. The defendant, however, knowingly waives the right to appeal and collaterally attack any component of a sentence imposed by the Court which falls within or is less than the sentencing range for imprisonment, a fine and supervised release set forth in Section III, § 15, above, notwithstanding the manner in which the Court determines the sentence. In the event of an appeal of the defendant's sentence by the government, the defendant reserves the right to argue the correctness of the defendant's sentence.

23. The defendant understands that by agreeing to not collaterally attack the sentence, the defendant is waiving the right to challenge the sentence in the event that in the future the defendant becomes aware of previously unknown facts or a change in the law which the defendant believes would justify a decrease in the defendant's sentence.

24. The government waives its right to appeal any component of a sentence imposed by the Court which falls within or is greater than the sentencing range for imprisonment, a fine and supervised release set forth in Section III, § 15, above, notwithstanding the manner in which the Court determines the sentence. However, in the event of an appeal from the defendant's sentence by the defendant, the government reserves its right to argue the correctness of the defendant's sentence . . .

APPENDIX B

I was compelled to include the response from the government here concerning my 2255 Motion, not because most readers will find it interesting. On the contrary, most will find it extremely complex and boring to read. But I still have high hopes that a lawyer who specializes in constitutional law will pick it up and realize the system has fallen to desperate new depths, and the integrity of our judicial system, in general, is in grave jeopardy.

LEGAL STANDARD
Effect of guilty plea and waiver of appeal

7. The petitioner's plea agreement, at paragraph 22, contained a waiver of appeal, effective so long as the defendant was sentenced within the range of 15–21 months. [See, Plea agreement at Docket Entry #85]. The petitioner was sentenced within the range (18 months). Generally, where a defendant, as in this case, pleads guilty unconditionally while represented by counsel and has a waiver of appeal, the defendant is barred from raising on appeal any issues occurring prior to the plea, specifically including alleged speedy trial violations. United States v. Parisi, 529 F.3d 134, 138 (2nd Cir. 2008). "To raise a claim despite a guilty plea or appeal waiver, the petitioner

must show that the plea agreement was not knowing and voluntary, <u>United States v. Da Cai Chen,</u> 127 F.3d 286, 289–90 (2d Cir.1997), because 'the advice he received from counsel was not within acceptable standards,' <u>United States v. Torres,</u> 129 F.3d 710, 715–16 (2d Cir.1997)." <u>Parisi,</u> *supra*, at 138.

Ineffective assistance of counsel

8. A defendant's right to counsel as guaranteed by the Sixth Amendment "is the right to effective assistance of counsel." <u>McMann v. Richardson,</u> 397 U.S. 759, 771, n.14; (1970) <u>Strickland v. Washington,</u> 466 U.S. 668, 686 (1984). To establish a claim that counsel was constitutionally ineffective, a defendant "must show both that his counsel's performance was deficient as measured by objective professional standards, and that this deficiency prejudiced his defense." <u>Purdy v. United States,</u> 208 F.3d 41, 44 (2d Cir. 2000); <u>Strickland,</u> 466 U.S. at 687; <u>Chang v. United States,</u> 250 F.3d 79, 84 (2d Cir. 2001).

9. The Supreme Court has "'declined to articulate specific guidelines for appropriate attorney conduct,'" instead emphasizing that "'the proper measure of attorney performance remains simply reasonableness under prevailing professional norms,'" <u>Wiggins v. Smith,</u> 539 U.S. 510, 523 (2003) (quoting <u>Strickland,</u> 466 U.S. at 688–89), which requires "a context-dependent consideration of the challenged conduct as seen 'from counsel's perspective at the time.'" <u>Wiggins,</u> 539 U.S. at 521 (quoting <u>Strickland,</u> 466 U.S. at 688).

10. When addressing the first prong of the <u>Strickland</u> ineffectiveness test, namely whether counsel's assistance

was deficient, the court must determine whether counsel's assistance was reasonable in light of all of the circumstances, and because of the difficulties in making this evaluation, the court must indulge a strong presumption that counsel's conduct fell within the wide range of reasonable professional assistance. In other words, the defendant must overcome the presumption that the challenged action might be considered sound trial strategy. The second prong of the Strickland test focuses on whether counsel's deficient performance rendered a result of the trial unreliable or the proceeding fundamentally unfair.

11. Under Strickland's standard for evaluating ineffective assistance of counsel claims, judicial scrutiny of a counsel's performance must be highly deferential, and every effort must be made to eliminate the distorting effects of hindsight, to reconstruct the circumstances of counsel's challenged conduct, and to evaluate the conduct from counsel's perspective at the time. Bell v. Cone, 535 U.S. 685, 698 (2002). "It is all too tempting for a defendant to second-guess counsel's assistance after conviction or adverse sentence, and it is all too easy for a court, examining counsel's defense after it has proved unsuccessful, to conclude that a particular act or omission of counsel was unreasonable." Id. It is well-established that actions or omissions by counsel that "might be considered sound trial strategy" do not constitute ineffective assistance. Michel v. Louisiana, 350 U.S. 91, 101, (1955); United States v. Berkovich, 168 F.3d 64, 67 (2d Cir. 1999); Mason v. Scully, 16 F.3d 38, 42 (2d Cir. 1994).

ARGUMENT

I. THE DEFENDANT'S PLEA OF GUILTY AND WAIVER OF APPEAL BARS CONSIDERATION OF HIS REQUEST FOR RELIEF

12. In his motion, the petitioner faults his counsel for not seeking dismissal of the Indictment during the pendency of the case. The defendant laments that his counsel did not address either the statute of limitations or speedy trial issue prior to the commencement of trial and his plea of guilty. However, the petitioner has failed to allege or set forth facts suggesting that his plea of guilty was not knowing or voluntary based on the alleged insufficiencies of his legal representation. Thus, in light of the petitioner's plea of guilty and waiver of appeal, the Court should summarily dismiss the petition. However, in the event the Court opts to consider petitioners claims, the government urges the Court to dismiss the petition based on the arguments set forth below.

II. THE STATUTE OF LIMITATIONS OFFERS NO REMEDY IN THIS CASE

13. Petitioner argues that his counsel was ineffective in failing to move for dismissal of Count 1 (theft from an employee benefit plan) because the prosecution of that charge was barred by the five-year statute of limitation of Title 18, United States Code, Section 3282. Petitioner's claim is without merit and should be denied.

14. First, the petitioner was not convicted under Count 1 of the indictment. In fact, Count 1 was dismissed following his plea and sentence under Counts 3 and 63 of the Indictment. Accordingly, the defendant was not

prejudiced by the perceived oversight of the petitioner's counsel in not moving to dismiss Count 1.

15. Second, the petitioner and his counsel signed a written waiver of the statute of limitations during the pre-indictment phase of the case which defeats his statute of limitations claim. Attached hereto exhibit A is the waiver of the statute of limitations signed by the petitioner and his counsel on December 8, 2006. The waiver barred a statute of limitations defense for any offense not barred prior to June 30, 2006, for a period of one year from that date, namely, June 29, 2007. A waiver of the statute of limitations defense is enforceable against a defendant. United States v. Cote, 544 F.3d 88, 103 (2nd Cir. 2008); United States v. Flood, 635 F.3d 1255, 1258 (10th Cir. 2011): United States v. Helblinq, 209 F.3d 226, 236 (3rd Cir. 2000).

16. The conduct alleged in Count 1 of the Indictment took place between on or about December 2001, through on or about January 9, 2002. Thus, absent a waiver, the statute of limitations as to Court 1 would have expired on January 9, 2007. However, by terms of the signed waiver, the statute of limitations period was extended until June 29, 2007. The original Indictment was returned on June 26, 2007, before the expiration of the agreed upon extension of the statute of limitations.

17. Based on the foregoing, the petitioner's claim that his counsel was ineffective for failing to seek dismissal of Count 1 of the Superseding Indictment based on a statute of limitations violation should be denied.

III. THE FAILURE OF COUNSEL TO MOVE FOR DISMISSAL OF THE SUPERSEDING INDICTMENT

BASED ON A SPEEDY TRIAL CLAIM DID NOT
CONSTITUTE INEFFECTIVE ASSISTANCE OF
COUNSEL

A. The Superseding Indictment reset the Speedy
Trial Clock

18. In his motion, the petitioner cites several periods
of delay as violating the Speedy Trial Act. A number of
the challenged periods occurred during the pendency of
the original indictment. The government will not address
those periods because the filing of the Superseding
Indictment on December 18, 2007, which added more
health care fraud counts and included, for the first time,
tax fraud counts, commenced a new Speedy Trial clock.
See, United States v. Deas, 596 F.Supp.2d 319, 323
(D.Conn., 2009) ("However, it is also well-settled that a
superseding indictment issued more than thirty days after
a defendant's arrest and adding a new charge to those
contained in the complaint and the original indictment
does not violate the Speedy Trial Act."); United States v.
Laqasse, 2005 WL 2620598 (D.Vt. 2005) (Where
superseding indictment is filed adding new charges, the
speedy trial clock is reset); United States v. Lattany, 982
F.2d 866, 873 n. 7 (3d Cir.1992) ("When subsequent
charges are filed in a supplemental indictment that charge
the same offense as the original indictment or one
required to be joined therewith, as in this case, the speedy
trial period commences with the original filing. If the
subsequent filing charges a new offense that did not have
to be joined with the original charges, then the subsequent
filing commences a new, independent speedy trial
period," citing United States v. Ramos, 588 F.Supp. 1223,
1226–27 (S.D.N.Y.1984), aff'd, 779 F.2d 37 (2d Cir.

1985).

19. Based on the foregoing, because the Superseding Indictment contained new offenses, the Speedy Trial was reset at 70 days remaining upon the filing of the Superseding Indictment.

B. Defense Counsel's failure to file a Speedy Trial motion relative to the Superseding Indictment was not faulty given the case law at the time

20. Petitioner claims that the delay in bringing his case to trial violated the Speedy Trial Act and, that in failing to bring a motion to dismiss on Speedy Trial grounds, his counsel was ineffective. The petitioner is wrong. As set forth below, the periods of delay properly were excluded from Speedy Trial Act calculations based on the then current case law. Because the Speedy Trial Act was not violated, the petitioner's claim for relief must be denied.

21. Attached as Exhibit B is the time line of the proceedings in this case subsequent to the filing of the Superseding Indictment. Exhibit B sets forth each period of delay in bringing the Superseding Indictment to trial and delineates the Court's findings regarding Speedy Trial Act exclusions for those delays.

22. On October 28, 2009, during the pendency of the Superseding Indictment, the Second Circuit issued a decision in United States v. Oberoi, 547 F.3d 436 (2nd Cir. 2008). In Oberoi, at 450–51, the Second Circuit, in upholding the decision of the District Court in the United States v. Oberoi, 295 F.Supp.2d 286, 295 (W.D.N.Y. 2003), joined a majority of circuit courts in holding that time excluded for the preparation of motions is automatically excluded for Speedy Trial Act purposes pursuant to motion exclusion of 18 U.S.C. 3161(h)(1)(F).

The Second Circuit ruled that the Speedy Trial Act did not require an express interest of justice finding for delay attributable to the preparation of motions. This standard remained law in the Second Circuit until March 8, 2010, Supreme Court decision in Bloate v. United States, 559 U.S.__, 130 S.Ct. 1345, three days after the petitioner's guilty plea in the instant case.

23. In a case directly on point, Parisi v. the United States, 529 F.3d 134, 141 (2nd Cir. 2008), the Second Circuit found that counsel's failure to bring a Speedy Trial motion, based on the state of the Speedy Trial case law at the time, was not ineffective, even if such a motion might have prevailed under subsequent case law developments: "Under Strickland, we must 'consider the circumstances counsel faced at the time of the relevant conduct', Davis U, 428 F.3d 81, 88, and Parisi has not persuaded us that his attorney erred in not anticipating such a development in the law." Parisi, id.

24. In the instant case, the only period of time after the filing of the Superseding Indictment that was not excluded pursuant to an express interest of justice finding or by the actual filing of motions was the time period from January 10, 2008, through April 29, 2008 (more than the 70 days permitted to bring the Indictment to trial; see paragraph b in Government Exhibit B attached hereto). This period of time was to be utilized by the defense for the preparation of motions, and pursuant to the docket entry for January 10, 2008, [Docket Entry #14] and the written Speedy Trial Order (Docket Entry #43], was excluded from the Speedy Trial clock solely by the motion provision of 18 U.S.C. 3161(h)(1)(F). There was not an interest of justice finding under 18 U.S.C. 3161(h)

(8)(A) for that exclusion.

25. In the instant case, the exclusion of the motion preparation period (January 10, 2008, through April 29, 2008) under the motion provision of 18 U.S.C. 3161(h)(1)(F) was consistent with the then valid Second Circuit case law as established in the <u>Oberoi</u> decisions. Although the Supreme Court, in <u>Bloate,</u> ruled to the contrary only three days after the petitioner's guilty plea in this case and would have made a motion to dismiss on the petitioner's behalf viable, the petitioner's counsel could not reasonably have been expected to anticipate such a decision. This is especially true because, as noted by the Supreme Court in <u>Bloate,</u> supra at 1351, eight of the Circuit Courts had issued decisions on the issue that were consistent with <u>Oberoi,</u> and only two had ruled to the contrary.

26. Given that petitioner's potential motion to dismiss the Superseding Indictment would have been denied under the then existing case law, and his counsel had no reason to expect the law in this area would change, the petitioner's motion to dismiss for ineffective assistance of counsel should bedenied, consistent with <u>Parisi v. the United States,</u> 529 F.3d 134, 141 (2nd Cir. 2008).

The delay in the filing of the written Speedy Trial Orders is of no consequence

[So what we get from this previous government statement is that, if I had stayed in the game just three more days, at that point my appeal would have been granted because my lawyers would have been ineffective due to the Bloate decision. And why isn't it something my lawyers brought up a week after my plea?]

27. Throughout his motion, the petitioner, citing United States v. Tunnessen, 763 F.2d 74 (2nd Cir. 1985), claims that many of the Speedy Trial Orders were improperly granted *nun pro tunc* because the written orders were filed on May 12, 2008, many months after the periods of time they excluded for Speedy Trial purposes. The defendant is wrong.

28. As set forth in the attached schedule of exclusions (Exhibit B), the Court made contemporaneous findings regarding the Speedy Trial Act exclusions, as reflected in each of the docket entries. Tunnessen, *supra*, at 78 and 79, clearly holds that so long as the reason for the prospective exclusion is set forth at the time it is granted, the Court may later expand its reasoning:

Accordingly, we conclude that time may not be excluded based on the ends-of-justice unless the District Court indicates at the time it grants the continuance that it is doing so upon a balancing of the factors specified by section 3161(h)(8). We also adopt the position taken in other circuits that the precise reasons for the decision need not be entered on the record at the time the continuance is granted. See United States v. Brooks, 697 F.2d 517 at 522 (citing cases). A prospective statement that time will be excluded based on the ends of justice serves to assure the reviewing court that the required balancing was done at the outset. Moreover, it puts defense counsel on notice that the Speedy Trial Clock has been stopped. If for any reason counsel believes that this is inappropriate, an objection may be raised, and a record made at that time. In any event, a later recording of the precise findings required by the Act will in most cases provide the reviewing court with an adequate record for review. We emphasize, of course, that where possible "a court generally should make the findings required by section 3161(h)(8)(A) at the time it grants the continuance." United States v. Clifford, 664 F.2d 1090, 1095 (8th Cir.1981).

29. Based on the foregoing, the Court's contemporaneous findings granting prospective Speedy Trial Act exclusions, as noted in the minutes, and as later memorialized in formal Orders, were proper. Thus, a motion to dismiss the Superseding Indictment pursuant to reasoning in Tunnessen properly would have been denied. Accordingly, defense counsel was not ineffective for failing to file such a motion. For this reason, petitioner's request for relief must be denied.

The petitioner failed to establish that he was prejudiced even if the Superseding Indictment would have been subject to dismissal.

30. Even if the Indictment had been subject to dismissal on Speedy Trial grounds, the petitioner failed to show that such a dismissal would have been with prejudice. Having failed in this regard, the petitioner's claim for relief must be denied.

31. The Second Circuit decision in Oberoi, 2010 WL 2135647 (2nd Cir. 2010) set forth the standard for determining whether a Speedy Trial should be with or without prejudice:

"In determining whether to dismiss the case with or without prejudice, the court shall consider, among others, each of the following factors: the seriousness of the offense; the facts and circumstances of the case which led to the dismissal; and the impact of a reprosecution on the administration of this chapter and on the administration of justice." 18 U.S.C. § 3162(a)(1). "[T]here is no presumption in favor of dismissal with prejudice in this circuit." Simmons, 786 F.2d 479 at 485.

"Where the crime charged is serious, the sanction of dismissal with prejudice should ordinarily be imposed only for serious delay." *Id.* The remaining considerations also weigh towards dismissal without prejudice, as "this case did not involve intentional non-compliance with the Act, nor was it designed to gain a tactical advantage for the government [,] . . . [and Oberoi] has not presented evidence of prejudice." *Id.* at 485–86.

Oberoi, *id.*

32. In the instant case, as in Oberoi, the charges were serious. Here, the petitioner was charged with theft from an employee benefit plan, health care fraud, and tax fraud. The petitioner received a sentence of 18 months imprisonment and was ordered to pay $127,804.87 in restitution. Given the seriousness of the charges as reflected in the Court's sentence, the petitioner, in order to have the Superseding Indictment dismissed with prejudice, would have to show not only serious delay but establish the government was solely responsible for the delay and that it gained a tactical advantage by intentional non-compliance. Petitioner has not, and could not, meet that burden. Thus, the petitioner's request for relief must be denied.

CONCLUSION

For all the foregoing reasons, the petitioner's request that the Court vacate his judgment of conviction and dismiss the Superseding Indictment should in all respects be denied.

ACKNOWLEDGMENTS

There are many thanks I would like to give to those who have given me unconditional love and friendship throughout my life and inspired and helped me during the writing of this book.

My parents have always been the foundation of our entire family, and their love and support provided me with the strength and determination to work hard at whatever we did—and to end each day feeling that we "amounted to something."

My wife, Larina, and my three sons, Stone, Myles, and Thorne, lived this ordeal with me, and without our unwavering love for one another, the lives that we lead today would not have been possible.

To everyone who has offered me an encouraging word throughout this legal ordeal, I want to say thank you! Kind words really do make more of a difference than we realize.

And without Steve Eggleston, the telling of my story would have been impossible. Steve was able to organize my thoughts through months of conversation, giving me direction and purpose, and, when writing became too hard for me to manage, he had the patience to help me through the project. To my friend, Steve, thank you so much!

Wise words of encouragement from a wise man:

"Do you think you'll ever amount to anything?"
-    RICHARD I GEISE

ABOUT THE AUTHOR

DR. SCOTT GEISE is a dentist, a US Army War Veteran, and an Amazon best-selling author with his debut work entitled *A Disturbing Injustice*. His passion has always been serving his patients and community through dentistry, but when afforded the time to write, he has found another way to serve.

He wrote dozens of articles for the local newspapers reflecting his interest in the rich history surrounding the Erie Canal. Through countless hours of research, he has uncovered an incredible industrial past that very few realized ever existed. His historical knowledge led to the formation of a non-profit organization called the Historic Lockport Mill Race that continues to promote local tourism in Lockport, New York.

A Disturbing Injustice reflects the need for accountability within our legal system and demonstrates in real life what can happen to a productive member of society when lies, greed, and power unexpectedly knock on the door.

Determined to remain optimistic and happy, he lives with his lovely wife and boys amongst the beautiful fruit orchards of a quaint little town called Newfane.

Made in United States
North Haven, CT
30 November 2024

61147581R00171